The Christian Art of

VERBAL CHESS

The Christian Art of

VERBAL CHESS

Speaking Life into Others

DAVID M. HOWARD

FOXH♦LE
M I N I S T R Y

www.foxholeministry.com

About the Author

David Howard is a Montana State Senator. He is a minister, founder of Foxhole Ministry, and creator of the national radio program "The Voice of Truth's Wake-up Call" which is broadcast daily in twenty-two states.

David is a regionally known speaker and presenter of educational topics such as The Culture War on Christianity, The Theology of Liberty, and Christ in Politics. A former FBI agent, he's an authority on workplace violence prevention and created the training program "Art of Verbal Chess" that provides the tools to become a Master Communicator.

David is a Certified Fraud Examiner and Expert Witness. He holds a master's degree in Public Management from DePaul University, and a bachelor's degree in Criminology from California State University, Los Angeles.

David's previous authorships include the non-fiction, *Attack on Christianity* and a Christian historical fiction book, *The Story of Eternal Life*.

He is married to Carla and they have six daughters and seventeen grandchildren.

Other Books by David Howard

Attack on Christianity

The Story of Eternal Life

These books as well as David Howard's timely and thought-pro-voking blog are available at www.foxholeministry.com where you can also download Foxhole Ministry's mobile app for Android or iPhone.

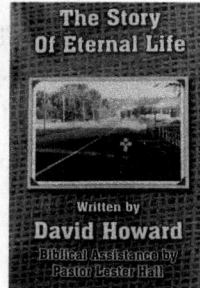

Contents

Introduction

TO BE EFFECTIVE communicators for Christ we must have a proven strategy. We have all had experiences where we have kept our mouths shut and been thankful for it, or we have verbalized the greatest comeback and made the whole world envious. We have also wished we could have said something but did not know the "Art of Speaking Life into Others." Are these situations fortunate, planned, lucky, or caused by a lack of a verbal strategy? Many of these situations are usually never planned. They are also unpredictable. Therefore, we need a system or a *strategy* to diffuse verbal conflict and edify meaningful conversation to speak life into others. This is why we want to learn the game of the Master Communicator, the Christian Art of Verbal Chess.

The proven goal of Verbal Chess is to learn a system that enables us to fruitfully move through the verbal mine field of life, and to respond appropriately and effectively every time. In this book, we are going to learn a system of communication called the Christian Art of Verbal Chess. Just as in any game, there are "pieces" that each have a function and must be mastered in order for us to succeed. The following are the pieces of the game.

Introduction

KING—The Persona of Verbal Chess—On the Christian Art of Verbal Chess side of the playing field, the King is the mind and nature, the moral compass, and the inner truth of who we really are. The King exemplifies ten essential character disciplines necessary to win life's game of communication. Emboldened by these character disciplines the King designs the strategy and directs the pieces where they will do the most good.

QUEEN—The Skill of Giving Grace—The Queen is our most versatile piece and the most difficult to learn to use skillfully. The Queen works from within every piece on the Christian Art of Verbal Chess side of the playing field. Truly the spirit of the game, it is the power to impartially step into another's life, seeing the world through their eyes, and then selflessly giving mercy and compassion to gain understanding, while being able to step back and see the reality of the circumstances.

BISHOPS—Empathic Listening—The Bishop is our intelligence gatherer, our unnatural, highly artistic tool to read our opponent. The Bishop can move diagonally across the playing field to search, anticipate, and understand our opponent's most important inner feelings.

KNIGHTS—Strategic Speaking—The Knight is our verbal personality and is the most unique motion piece of the game. It moves over or around our opponent to truthfully influence them. The Knight can be the key to success or an avenue to failure when playing the Christian Art of Verbal Chess.

CASTLES—Silent Communication—The Castle is our silent vehicle of communication to understand what is *not* spoken and influence our opponent covertly. It also moves forward and backward, side-to-side, changing the playing field by presenting different views of our inner self and outward demeanor.

PAWNS—Our On-Time Delivery Techniques—Pawns use all the pieces of the game to move our opponent to persuasion or compliance through compelling, and positive influences on-time. Pawns move forward one space at a time. They can be calming, persuasive, protective, and assuring, but they don't move back. Pawns are created and delivered through our body language, tone of voice, personal space, and our words, while working in harmony with our mind, mouth, and body.

Winning the game of communication in our everyday lives is paramount in developing successful relationships. Building thriving relationships is the secret to success in all facets of life, including family, business, and especially discipleship. The answer to building thriving relationships is an affirming, constructive, and edifying communication that harmonizes our mind, mouth, and body. This is truly one of life's greatest gifts and challenges. This is the Christian Art of Verbal Chess, the Art of Speaking Life into Others.

1

The Beginning

WHEN I WAS a young military policeman in Korea, I grasped for any communication tool I could find (but at the time they were nowhere to be found). I was helpless and at times felt as though I was drowning and personally lacking in intelligence. One night, I was on walking patrol in the village of Sin Chon Dong (the sin is very appropriate) and an incident took place that showed how much I needed communication skills. I had to rely on trickery and brute force to obtain compliance and solve a dangerous adversarial confrontation.

The situation arose when I encountered a big GI who was drunk, stoned, and very mad. He felt the Dream Boat Club had somehow collaborated with a "moose" (the GI's name for a prostitute) to steal his money he had left on the table. He grabbed a waitress as she walked by, broke a bottle, and held it to her face demanding his money.

A young Korean boy ran down the alley toward us yelling, "Big trouble, big GI hurting people!" I was a newly arrived military policeman on one of my first walking patrols. I was with Allen, an "old guy," an MP who had been in Korea only about six months. He followed me as we walked through the back door of the Dream Boat Club. The reason the "old guys" always followed the new guys, was because it was safer to be second while walking into a bar.

Inside, I observed that troublemaker with sweat running down his forehead and beading on his arm which he held around the young woman's neck. The waitress was staring at me with eyes that were pleading for help, and because she was short, she was bent backward with her feet barely touching the floor. The hardwood bar was behind him, and as usual the prostitutes lined the wall, seemingly unconcerned. The bar was half full of GIs in varying stages of drunkenness, watching and laughing. I somehow remember the song that was playing, "A Whiter Shade of Pale," and when someone turned it off, the GIs booed.

The little Korean who ran the joint, ran up and kept saying, "No trouble, no trouble, I will get your money."

Allen said, "I know this guy! He is going to cut her and fight us."

The GI looked like a crazed animal, as I walked within six feet of him with both of my arms out to the side, and hands palms up not knowing what to say or do.

I sputtered, "All right it's over! Put the bottle down and I'll make sure you get your money, okay?"

"%&@! you! I hate these mother-%&@!ing gooks. I could kill them all," he yelled. I could see his eyes were wild and his face had a mean look.

I saw the fear in the waitress's face as her eyes were staring towards the broken bottle now pressing against her face. I felt like I had to do something quickly or this waitress was going to bleed. What could I say?

"Hey look!" I said as I reached into my back pocket and pulled out my wallet. I was trying to slow things down, but everything was moving in a blur. I showed him my wallet and immediately threw it to him with my left hand, shouting, "I'll buy this one from you."

The Beginning

I was hoping he was right-handed and would instinctively try to catch the wallet with the hand holding the bottle.

It seemed like everything was in slow motion when I saw his eyes following the wallet in the air. I started pulling my black plastic nightstick from its holder with my right hand, rushing toward him at the same moment the GI's hand moved from her face towards the wallet. Remarkably, he used two fingers to catch the wallet still holding the bottle. This was lucky for the waitress! My timing was almost perfect. I hit his hand as he caught the wallet, smashing the bottle in his hand with my nightstick.

The GI grimaced, turning slightly to the left looking at his hand. In that moment, I could see blood appear on the palm of his hand as I was surging ahead. The big GI staggered backwards, letting go of the waitress as he was grabbing for his right hand with his left hand. I slightly turned as I crashed into him with my shoulder, like a linebacker taking a running back. I could briefly smell his beer breath as we separated and sprawled on the floor.

Allen was immediately on top of the GI cocking his 1911 .45 pistol with his left hand and pointing it at the GI's face. The guy groaned.

Allen yelled, "Turn over, you mother %&@!er."

The GI looked at the .45 two inches from his nose, and slowly turned over. He was now as docile as a little lamb. Allen put handcuffs on him and looked at me with a big smile as I got up off the floor. The GIs in the bar were cheering like we just won a football game. I looked around at the waitress and she was rubbing her face but there was no blood. I was extremely thankful as I stood looking over at Allen. "What?"

"%&@!ing bad man. You are %&@!ing bad!"

"Me?" I thought to myself, smiling at Allen, but kind of not liking the compliment. Later, I knew there must have been something I could have tried other than trickery and brute force. I thought I could have negated the extreme risks of this encounter, using something other than what I'd used.

Little did I know, there were a multitude of things I could have tried during this encounter. The trouble was, not only did I not know what to try, I did not know what had really happened which caused the situation to deteriorate so quickly. Could I have changed the tempo by maybe showing less aggressive body language? Could I have just pulled out a chair and sat down to hear what he had to say? Could I have made everyone in that bar leave and therefore slowed the process? This is an example of how we can fail at communication because we do not have the slightest idea what to do.

Later when I was a new FBI agent in Montana and assigned to cover two Indian reservations, I discovered a much better way to handle stressful situations. I got a call about midnight from the Indian reservation, advising that earlier that evening a male was murdered in his home while he slept with his wife. They were requesting my help. Upon arrival, my crime scene investigation revealed the murderer came through the back door of the home, grabbed a butcher knife out of the kitchen drawer, proceeded into the bedroom, and stabbed the husband while he was in the bed with his wife. The husband fought off the attacker, escaped through the bedroom window, where he collapsed and died, about thirty yards from the house. The wife was not harmed.

Interviews of the neighbors revealed the suspect was the wife's boyfriend. The Indian police told me the wife/girlfriend was in jail because she did not cooperate. I proceeded to the jail and the Crow

Indian police told me with a sneer, "She's from the Dog family."
"The Dog family?" Apparently, she was Northern Cheyenne, and
the Cheyenne and the Crow Indians are ancient enemies. Could
one tribe have a little vendetta against the other? Absolutely! Do
you think I was almost in a foreign land within my own country?
Yes, I was! Who do you think she might dislike a little more than
the Crow police? You got it—this young, white FBI agent, the one
with the sports coat and tie at 5 a.m.

The Crow police told me, "There's no way she's talking to
you. No way!"

"Okay," I said, "but I have to try."

She was sitting in the jail cell on a bunk without a mattress. I
asked the jailer, "How long has she been here?" "Five hours." I was
thinking: the murder took place about eleven o'clock; somebody
called me about midnight; I'm here and it's about five o'clock in the
morning; and she has been sitting here all that time. I wondered
if she had had anything to drink or eat. So, I walked in, sat down,
and introduced myself. She didn't even acknowledge that I was in
the same world. Plus, I had another problem.

The odor was tremendously bad in the jail cell, reeking of urine
and the body odor of this woman who smelled like she probably
hadn't taken a bath in a month. I was almost overcome by the
smell. At that point, I said, "I'll be right back." I got up and walked
into the other room, gasping, trying to get fresh air, and trying to
get the fortitude to go back in there. I said a little prayer: Lord,
I need your help. Then an idea hit me. I put some quarters into
some vending machines. Out came a couple sodas and chips. I
was hoping the taste of the soda and the smell of the chips would
dilute the urine and body odor. I walked back in there trying not
to take a breath. I set her soda and chips on a stool next to her by

the steel bed. Nodding toward her I open my soda and at first tried to smell the chips, but now the potato chip smell combined with the smell of urine and BO. I started drinking and eating, hoping I wouldn't gag. She looked down, picked up her food, and then looked at me. A small smile crossed her face for just an instant, and she started drinking and eating.

I waited for a few moments then just started talking. "I'm sorry I have to bother you tonight." She looked at me but her face didn't show any emotion. I said, "You know I haven't been in Montana very long." I told her a short story about my family and my life. I had no idea what I was doing. I was just fishing. I was grabbing for straws, a proverbial shot in the dark, so to speak. How do I talk to this person? How do I treat her? What should be my countenance? She is on the other side of the world from me culturally, and I don't think I can relate to her. I don't even want to be there because of the smells and everything else that is repulsive to me. I had the urge to walk out and dry heave.

I started this conversation that turned out to be a short story about myself because of my uncomfortable situation. To my surprise, she began talking about her childhood. I asked short, open-ended questions about her life and I listened. During this listening period, I started to mentally step into her life seeing the world through her eyes, giving a kind of grace. Grace is mercy and forgiveness. Mercy, because in my heart of hearts I thought she didn't deserve this time I was giving her, and forgiveness because at that moment I believed she may have helped kill her husband. But without grace, all rolled into mercy and forgiveness, I was not going to be able to continue the interview with her.

She told me how she grew up under a bar stool at the Jim Town Bar. When she was thirteen years old she was an alcoholic and had been raped several times by an uncle. Her mother was a drunk, and she did not know her father. She married her husband, who was a Crow, at age fifteen to get away from her uncle.

I couldn't help it, but I felt so sorry for her. I kept telling myself to step back emotionally, and don't get too involved in her story. When she finished, I went and got her another coke and chips and set them down before her. I didn't know what to say so I said nothing. I sort of sat there looking at my feet and occasionally looking into her eyes, nodding at her, as if to say I understood, showing a great amount of empathy. She finally wiped the tears from her eyes and looked up at me with an inquiring look and said, "You want to know what happen?" I nodded.

She then told me she was the girlfriend of the killer but had no previous knowledge of the attack and witnessed the whole thing. She said she would testify if need be. I then obtained a signed statement and was able to prove this murder case against the boyfriend.

I had succeeded, but what did I do? Could I repeat it? Truthfully, as I left the jail the Crow police jokingly accused me of being a con man or a trickster! One said, "You're really smooth!" I shook my head and said, "Only a little kindness." But was it just kindness, or could this have been only partially responsible? Was it the listening? Was it my demeanor or countenance? Was it the distance I sat from her? Was it because I truly felt sorry for her? Was it because I provided the chips and soda? Later I would discover I used communication the right way and knew the other situation in the bar was the wrong method.

Later I created an FBI interviewing program that I could teach at police schools. The program used on-time symptom techniques to determine if the subject of the interview was telling the truth.

On-time means an immediate first response, thereby creating a system to judge the interviewee's truthfulness. These symptom techniques were built around certain types of questions, reading body language, and noting on-time body language responses. This was very effective and gave the interviewer several tools to use. This program provided a significant advantage over the training I'd received in the FBI at that time. I had been taught not ask leading questions, and of course, there are times when leading questions are exactly what we needed to ask.

Years after being an FBI agent, obtaining a master's degree, creating, developing, and eventually selling my investigative firm, I started a consulting/training firm. One of my clients was a fire district which requested instruction on workplace violence prevention. A small portion of my course was dedicated to communication. Later a good friend, Fire Chief George Appel, after having their employees go through my Violence in the Workplace Prevention Training, asked me to put together a course that focused on communication. They wanted information which would teach fire inspectors how to communicate in conflict situations and obtain voluntary compliance. They wanted a comprehensive communication training program.

My goal was to identify the methodology of a Master Communicator and create a training program that would be easy for the students to learn and continue to practice. This turned out to be a whole lot easier said than done. It took longer and was much more difficult than expected. The process took many months of hard research, gathering results from my experiences, and writing and preparing the PowerPoint presentation. I concluded the best avenue was to teach communication as a strategy related to the game of chess, based on six comprehensive skills. The skills would be represented as chess pieces: the king, queen, bishop, knight, castle, and pawns. I hoped this would give the student the ability to see the big picture of communication and would make individual communication skills easier to learn so everyone—from the most intellectual to people like you and me—could learn to be Master Communicators.

The training was designed so the necessary tools of communication could continue to be practiced as we walked and ran through life. We could practice during our everyday experiences. This would help the player become better and better over the long term. Associating communication with chess would enable even those unfamiliar with the game to obtain useful, practical, strategic skills. Chess is a game of strategy just like all meaningful communication.

Chess is a game where we have to plan the strategy by creating tactics based on the ability of the pieces of the game. Every piece of the game of chess—as in the Christian Art of Verbal Chess—from the king to the pawns, is interrelated and dependent upon the other pieces in order to have success. In addition, once we realize all the parts or pieces of communication are dependent on each other, we can create more than a plan of action: we create a communication strategy. A strategy is much better than a plan because a strategy answers the question of why. Strategy has a larger opportunity to see the whole picture and define the end-result, identifying the many avenues to the desired outcome. A strategy looks at every possible influencing factor, both seen and unforeseen, and comes to terms with the whole situation, not just one result. This process was my breakthrough for learning to be a Master Communicator and develop the art of speaking life into others.

The Christian Art of Verbal Chess then becomes a learning process that helps us transcend the difficulties of learning communication by laying them out in front of us and simplifying them. We can now look down on the process of communication and see all the different pieces of the game we must master. This process empowers us to put tremendous value in our communication because now we can learn the game of communication in its entirety. Once we value this learning process, the Christian Art of Verbal Chess can become firmly ingrained in our persona, becoming almost second nature, and improving our ability to communicate with almost anyone. Then we can become Master Communicators and develop the art of speaking life into others as we continue to practice the game of communication every time we have meaningful conversations.

2

Who Are Master Communicators?

MASTER COMMUNICATORS ARE people who accomplish inward effectiveness and an incredible degree of outward achievement. This is what I call true success. They have an unusual nature—a selfless quality that draws people to them in unique ways. People admire them and wish they could be like them. Most of all, Master Communicators develop lasting friendships and loving family relationships because they develop the art of speaking life into others. They are the people who are married the longest, have the most friends, and are those who affirm others around them, which is truly a gift. They follow sound principles: "Let nothing be done through selfish ambition or conceit . . . Let each of you look out not only for his own interests, but also for the interests of others."[1] This is the key to success with the Christian Art of Verbal Chess.

In Verbal Chess these disciplines, traits, and skills, are practiced constantly and are continually developing. The Master Communicator is like a Chess Master. The Chess Master is one of the finest players even though he or she does not always win. The communication master is one of the best communicators, but neither can he or she stay on top of the game without constant practice. This practice is easier for communicators because they are applying their skills during every meaningful communication, which is done practically every waking hour of every day, with everyone they speak to.

There is one thing to keep in mind and never misunderstand. Masters of the Christian Art of Verbal Chess are not necessarily great orators or master debaters. These, in my experience, are different learned skills usually combined with special personalities. Master Communicators who adhere to Christ's truths have special natures and virtues. Their virtues come from the Book of Truth. To them, meaningful communication is an unselfish Christ-sponsored process, where they learn to be quick to listen, slow to speak, and slower to get angry.[2] The game of the Christian Art Verbal Chess is a win-win process and strategy whereby we become inflow enablers, strategic outflow experts, and never bow to verbal overflow. In other words, we enable others to communicate, we control what we communicate, and we never bloviate.

Strategic speaking and listening while reading others and controlling our body language, empowers us to become Master Communicators. This type of communication is all rolled into strategic thinking. This why the Christian Art of Verbal Chess is so successful: it simplifies the difficult. It takes complex issues of communication and long-term objectives that can be exceedingly difficult to address and breaks them down into manageable sizes.[3] The Book of Truth written over two thousand years ago confirms strategic thinking, "The plans of the diligent lead to profit as surely as haste leads to poverty."[4]

Strategic communication helps us to speak at the right times, listen like we are the most understanding person in the world, and ask the right questions on time, while keeping us from selfishly owning the process. This is so we can objectively view the subject matter from any angle, and answer who, what, where, how, and why. These might not be the only questions we are asked, or ask, but until we look at communication as a strategy, we will not likely get the answers or be able to communicate our solutions successfully. Strategic communication prepares us for the future.[5] None of us knows what tomorrow brings. Therefore, "Do not boast about tomorrow, for you do not know what a day may bring."[6]

This means strategic communication reduces the margin of error by not being self-serving. Uncontrolled speech, in my opinion, is self-serving speaking unless we are yelling, "Fire!" It can also be play-talking or conflict-talking. Uncontrolled speech is shooting from the hip, which greatly increases the margin of error. It is like a golfer misaligning a shot a few degrees off sending the ball onto the next fairway. Strategic communication lines up our actions with our honorable objectives, just as lining up a golf shot correctly helps us put the ball closer to the pin.[7] Strategic communication also gives us influence with others because it has both short-range and long-range objectives.[8]

A person once commented to me that his short-range plan was to get his way, and his long-range plan didn't matter. This is not strategic communication, because the person with the strategy is the person with the power of speaking life into others not death. Power, to one who practices the Christian Art of Verbal Chess, is always virtuous and never has unrighteous motives. Whatever type of communication we are involved in, Christ-based strategic communication is essential to being an effective honorable person because without a strategy we are controlled by happenstance and self-centeredness.

The minimum for success in the game of Christian Art of Verbal Chess is when the conversation is over and our opponent leaves; they may not have agreed with us or been persuaded, but they leave viewing us with respect. We cannot really control another person's thoughts, but we can speak and act in a respectable and righteous way. During encounters people can internally question our sincerity and our honesty. If we are honorable and gracious, they may not always like us or cherish our presence, but if we do not kill their liberty to speak and be heard, as they walk away, they will view us with respect. They respect us because they have been heard and affirmed by our attempt to understand them.

The motive of the Master Communicator is to speak like those "Who will be judged by the law that gives freedom."[9] This is when we give others the ability to speak and to be heard, which is to be affirmed—the supreme desire of every rational human. Case in point, is the Indian woman. When we are respected by others, we know we have gained mind, mouth, and body harmony by creating the freedom and liberty to communicate effectively. This is the minimum result we are seeking to win the Christian Art of Verbal Chess, the game of the Master Communicator, the art of speaking life into others.

3

The Verbal Chess Opponent

"WE HAVE FOUND the enemy and he are us," said by Pogo in the comic strip of the same name. Who is our opponent? Many times our opponent is us. Often when we fail at communication, we do so because we do not know how to play the game of life. This is why we desperately need to learn the Christian Art of Verbal Chess.

When we play Verbal Chess we must realize our opponent is someone we have a meaningful, friendly, or adversarial conversation with. Verbal Chess is not used when we are play-talking. Hence, the opponent can be anyone: ourselves, a co-worker, a subordinate, a superior, a sales prospect, or current client. The opponent can also be our spouse, children, family, friends, or someone we just met. Note, in the game of life our opponent is merely on the opposite side of the Verbal Chess game; we do not look upon them as our adversary. We may love them, dislike them, or have no feeling for them, but to have success in the game of life our motives are always founded in the persona of the King, and giving the grace of the Queen. Therefore, our opponent of Verbal Chess is called the Anti-King, Queen, Bishop, Knight, and Castle.

We are going to be challenged!

To play Verbal Chess and win, we must understand we are going to have a verbal chess opponent who can be negative and without hope or joy. They are the downside of communication. They will be the ones who verbally question, doubt, heckle, criticize, attack, lie, trick, con, and gossip about us. They are going to verbally challenge, persecute, or ostracize us. This is an absolute. Therefore, when we are under attack by someone who is playing verbal combat, if we do not maintain our self-control (which is our dignity and virtue) we cannot communicate powerfully. These givens help us accept the perimeters of the communication game of life. However, we can be emboldened to know, "Better is a poor man who walks in integrity than he who is perverse in speech and is a fool."[10]

The fact that we are going to be challenged is the same with almost any game or sport. In football years ago, I had to accept the given that it was going to hurt, and it was an absolute that if I did not control my fear of pain, I could not play effectively. Once I learned the pain was not going to kill me, I started to enjoy the game instead of fearing the pain. I could then focus on my play without worrying about the pain I was surely going to feel. It is the same with Verbal Chess. We must accept that other people will not play with dignity and virtue, and we must control our own attitudes, speech, and countenance to be effective. Therefore, if we cannot play the Christian Art of Verbal Chess with dignity and virtue, we can forget about effective communication. If we do not master our personal attributes, self, we will lose the game of Verbal Chess.

How do we prepare ourselves?
Control our intake!

To win at the game of Verbal Chess and continue to play, we have to play with dignity, virtue, and style. To accomplish this, we need to learn that we have to control our intake. Intake is what we take into our minds and into our hearts. There is an old saying, "A good man out of the good treasure of his heart brings forth good; and an evil man out of the evil treasure of his heart brings forth evil. For out of the abundance of the heart his mouth speaks."[11] Therefore, biblical intake is of paramount importance.

We store up what we let into our minds and humans emulate or act like what we have taken in. Intake becomes a major part of our personality because what goes in comes out in our countenance and speech. To prove this, all we have to do is look at unscrupulous people like Vladimir Lenin who focused on indoctrination and said, "Give me your four-year-olds, and in a generation I will build a socialist state." He did exactly that by controlling their intake and today we call it communism. Look what is happening with radical Muslims. Certain violent people are feeding their children hate and teaching them to justify killing non-Muslims from the very beginning of their lives. Even sixteen-year-old girls are blowing themselves up to kill innocents they have been taught to hate and kill. Their intake is hate and killing, and what comes forth is hate and killing. Likewise, if we surround ourselves or welcome the intake from people who lie and justify lying, like many of today's politicians and news outlets, we are vicariously being taught it is okay to lie and misrepresent truth to get what we want.

Look at the adverse effect on our children and others in this smart phone and iPad generation. They are being struck by instant stimulation that has little or no lasting value, and in the long-term

America's children are going to suffer. On the other hand, if we surround ourselves with honest godly people with positive Christian attributes, we will tend to adopt their model of honesty and positive attitudes. When we self-educate ourselves through sound biblical teaching, we tend to model ourselves after goodness and love. We then "hate evil; pride and arrogance, evil behavior and perverse speech."[12] This is critical when it comes to developing the character of dignity and virtue of a Master Communicator.

We must also to be able to put away our biases. But to do this we have to understand where they come from. There are two basic natures in all humans: *self* versus *selfless*. If we visualize a horizontal scale—to the extreme left is self and to the extreme right is selfless—we all live within this area. Depending on the subject, or the area of concern, we are all positioned somewhere between these two natures. On the far left side, we have a person totally focused on self and on the far right the totally unselfish. In our society we have an overabundance of people on the left who have a total self-focus.

The way of self is birthed in arrogance, molded in wants, needs, longings, and the development of every self-serving attribute. This is made evident by many book titles like *Looking out for #1*, focused on self and selling millions. Self without a greater God-sponsored purpose easily becomes the focus of human fantasies and can become habitual, self-serving attitudes in search of the next shiny object. Arrogance kills the strategic purpose in the game of the Christian Art of Verbal Chess.

I recently read a piece in the paper about an unmarried woman who was forty-two years old. She wrote the reason she never married was because she never met a man who fulfilled her needs. She probably never will because in successful marriages, we fulfill someone else's needs. Marriage, like all relationships, is not self-gratification, self-concern, self-indulgence, self-pleasure, and self-satisfaction or it is headed for divorce. It is the opposite. It is being more concerned for the other than we are for ourselves. It is the golden rule, to love others like you love yourself.[13]

To comprehend our selfishness we are born with it already established. Ask yourself: if someone is talking and the subject is interesting, and we want to say something, for whom are we saying it? If we dominate the conversation, do we feel good about the conversation? Chances are we do because we are satisfying our need to be heard, which is born in selfishness! If we are offended, are we focusing on self? If a person does something we perceive as letting us down, about whom are we concerned?

Self is the deep abyss of human nature. It is one of the most destructive tendencies and can lead us to an abundance of relationship failures. These stem from uncaring, selfish communication which is our opponent (though often that opponent is us). In other words, our nature is our roots which produce our branches. They are the way we learn to communicate, and the fruit that comes forth is what comes out of our mouths. Others judge us by the fruit we produce, but if our roots are bad, the branch bears bad fruit. The world does not see our roots or our branches; they see only the fruit we produce.

How do we move from the focus on self to selfless?

The selfish person in all of us is inclined toward winning the battle of communication by using either verbal manipulation or verbal abuse. Look at politics today. They are focused on smearing each other and cannot get along or have meaningful relationships with the other. When we use verbal manipulation or abuse, we lose in every other way. We play the age-old game of power and control and, in reality, we may gain temporary control but lose long-term respect. Therefore, eventually we lose all power over the relationship because humans learn to avoid relationships with arrogant, nasty people. Then we will not be respected or seen in a positive light; we may be feared or hated, but we will not be respected.

Self is one-dimensional with a fishbowl mentality. One-dimensional people are inside their self-made fishbowl; everything inside looks good to them, because what they see most of is their own reflection. Just like the woman who cannot find a husband to fit her needs. She saw her needs very clearly, but not the needs of a potential spouse. People who are afflicted with this kind of attitude are largely blinded by the effect of the fishbowl glass they live in. In reality, SELF blinds them.

The farther people move to the left of the scale of life—where bitter is called sweet and sweet, bitter—the more these people reinterpret everything for self, and the more they fail at communication. They do not understand why people outside their fishbowl do not accept or understand them. They lack the ability to see themselves and this becomes their shield from reality. This keeps them in their fishbowl of self-deceit. It prevents them from moving outside because this would reveal the truth that destroys their selfish vision. While shielding themselves from the truth, many take on the attitude of blamers, accusers, or self-professed victims (which are all related). These people are miserable. It is always sad to see people self-destruct, but one way or another, self, for these people, is their vehicle to destruction.

For proof look to a few who have self-destructed: The FBI agent who is now a traitor to his country, a past President who lied to his country and was impeached, a New York Senator who cannot run for office again because he took improper gifts and lied before Congress, the spouse who saw sexual conquest as more valuable than his relationship with his family. They all suffered from their actions born out of a self-serving attitude. Yes, many people thought they were special, some even had followers who admired them greatly. These types of people fool lots of others because they are actors and some are great orators with a public following. Some have fascinating outward personalities, but arrogance does them in.

Selflessness is the most powerful of all sustained influences

Master Communicators by their nature escape the abyss of arrogance in the game of life because they know it is how they affect others, the fruit they produce, that makes the difference. An absolute truth: You will know them by their fruits.[14]

Focusing on growing a selfless attitude forces us to begin the development of the inner traits and nature of the Master Communicator. Moving to selflessness forces us to see others with concern and compassion, and then and only then, can we start to see ourselves clearly and truthfully understand ourselves. We actually start looking in the mirror and saying, "Hmm, there are some problems here!" Once this takes place, we can begin to focus outwardly, and start making corrections in our behavior, thus focusing on being as concerned for others as we are for ourselves. We start to see the periphery, outside our focused inward vision. We climb out of our fishbowl and we start to see the joy and art of speaking life into others. This vision moves to the vast picture where we see ourselves in this universe and realize we are only one tiny living speck on one planet in an unlimited cosmic vastness.

We come to understand that selflessness is three-dimensional: others, reality, and then self. This panoramic view gives us humility and is very important for the normal development of all esteemed humans. Our beliefs, values, candor, and how we practice the unchangeable principles of life become self-evident. Selfless people are self-controlled, compassionate, kind, humble, gentle, and patient without seeking something in return.

Selfless is the direction we want to proceed, and it is not easy. It is an effort that starts every day and takes discipline to maintain. It is even interesting when we observe the reaction of people when they realize that someone is willing to do as much for others as they generally do for themselves.[15] Most people at first are disbelieving or suspecting. In such instances, many people are thinking unselfish people are wearing a mask; they must be hiding something, or they are up for promotion, or some other devious agenda. However, if our unselfishness is proven genuine there is no limit of reverence people are prepared to pay. This is the beautiful outcome for the Christian Art of Verbal Chess Communicator.

4

The King

THE NATURE OF VERBAL CHESS

THE KING IS the most important of all the players because the game starts and ends with the King's ten character disciplines. The King is not only the nature of the Verbal Chess side of the playing field, the King is our moral compass.

The King is the reflection of our virtues and our motives —our inner traits utilized in the game of Verbal Chess. These are simply the unchangeable qualities we should all live by, and they directly reflect our character because our motives become easily identified.

These *inner traits* are driven by ten disciplines: **integrity, self-control, humility, gratitude, acceptance, patience, forgiveness, faith, and hope, which all support the last trait, perseverance.**[16] We must constantly work on these disciplines to become the true reflection of the Christian Art of Verbal Chess. **Inner traits = our responses** to those people around us who are opponents in Verbal Chess. Also, these inner traits guide us during the uncontrollable events in our lives that cause conflict.

We need to understand, we all fall short while striving to build the nature of the King, but this is the point. The King is always striving to build and maintain these ten disciplines. William George Jordan said,

> Into the hand of every individual is given a marvelous
> power for good or evil. It's the silent, unconscious, unseen
> influence of our life. This is simply who we really are,
> not what we pretend to be. [17]

The adversary to the King in Verbal Chess is called the Anti-King. The Anti-King can be us. It sponsors communication warfare, versus the virtues of the King that enable us to destroy strongholds and "cast down arguments and every high thing that exalts itself."[18] The King does this by taking captive every perception and intention of the Anti-King and overcoming them. Through the King's nature our words and actions reveal honorable motives that conform to the disciplines of the King. It is then possible to not walk and talk according to the desires of the Anti-King. Instead, through our actions and speech we sponsor the nature of the King which is Jesus Christ within us.

The Anti-King

Do we wonder why people can't communicate in a positive or edifying way? Why are they so irritating, irksome, angry, and infuriating? Can they be momentarily filled with the dark side of humanity, the soul of the creature within all of us? For the purposes of Verbal Chess, we call this the Anti-King.

The Anti-King sponsors the inner rationalization of iniquity versus the virtues of goodness. The Anti-King side of Verbal Chess promotes the unwholesome motives contrary to everything the King of Verbal Chess stands for. They are in conflict with each other because on the Anti-King side of the game people say and do whatever comes into their minds. They are impatient, rude, harsh, and treat others in a surly manner. The Anti-King can go so far as to be mentally abusive, and obstinate. Many do this unknowingly because they have little or no self-control; their motives are self-serving.

The King's opponent, the Anti-King, is characterized by several creature traits: dishonesty, self-indulgence, arrogance, ingratitude, rejection, and revenge; they are all untrustworthy. They many times focus on blame and accusations, thereby creating a state of despair.[19]

The Anti-King, when it raises its ugly head during communication, is truly the killer of all good and reasonable communication. Productive communication goes into the trash heap because reason vanishes, objectivity is destroyed, and enriching dialog is finished. This proves the lie of the old saying, "Sticks and stones will break my bones, but names will never hurt me." Calling people names is mental abuse. It is accusing and blaming, which is speaking darkness into others. It has a devastating effect on relationships, self-esteem, and productivity. There is simply no profit in it.

I was watching a U.S. Congress hearing and a female U.S. Senator started the questioning by accusing the witness, America's Attorney General, of being a liar. Note, this is in America's Capitol where, by law, our Congress men and women and the U.S. Attorney General are called honorable. Honorable means they are entitled to the honor of respect, attesting to their credible conduct.

The Congresswoman started the questioning with a rant accusing and verbally abusing the witness. This is mental abuse and disparagement from a so-called honorable person to another honorable person. When the camera panned to the Attorney General, I could see the anger rising up in him. He kept his demeanor under control and replied in a respectful way. She was using Anti-King's trash talk in all its glory. From what was coming out of her mouth, she was showing the world on national TV she dwells in the valley of self-destruction. She was viewed as ethically lacking, a characterless persona, and devoid of a moral foundation.

This example should scare us to death if we want to be seen as honorable, good, and forthright. The key here is how we are seen as we communicate. No one viewing this Senator on national TV knew if she was a wonderful person or not. The outside world judges people on what comes out of their mouths. The Book of Truth defines these people this way:

> For they mouth empty, boastful words..., by appealing
> to the lustful desires of the flesh, they entice people who
> are just escaping from those who live in error.[20]

This kind of Anti-King speech, especially coming from people of authority—i.e., parents, pastors, teachers, and management—entices people who are struggling in the life of error, and negatively reinforces them to continue in error. This U.S. Senator should have been aware she was viewed as an authority figure, like parents, pastors, teachers, and management. She was supposed to an example of how to act and speak. She, because of her position, was seen as hiding behind her position of authority somehow self-condoning her behavior. The Book of Truth reveals who these kinds of people are,

> . . . evil smears among you, laughing and carrying on,
> gorging and stuffing themselves without a thought
> for others. They are like clouds blowing over dry land
> without giving rain, promising much, but producing
> nothing.[21]

The Ten Disciplines of the King

Integrity, Time-Tested Honesty

Without integrity we cannot have character because character is doing the right thing when no one is looking or will ever find out. These are people who when leaving a department store realize they were not charged for something and go back and say, "You didn't charge me for this."

Integrity is our persona's lifeblood. Without integrity we can't be truthful to ourselves or truthful to others. Being truthful to ourselves is what enables us to overcome failure because we see ourselves clearly in both the positive and negative. This enables us to correct ourselves. Being truthful to others gives us the ability to be seen as light in the world where darkness prevails. It's the living breath of virtue, and virtue births dignity, and dignity births self-respect. If we take away integrity, we lose our reason for being in the game of Verbal Chess, because ". . . integrity of the upright guides them, but the unfaithful are destroyed by their dishonesty."[22]

Psychological studies show that lying to ourselves is more deeply ingrained and harder to change than lying to others; it is almost impossible to cure. These self-liars tell themselves how they want to be; they look in the mirror, lie to themselves, and believe it is so. Self-truthfulness looks into the mirror, sees the areas to correct, and sets out to correct them. This inner trait of self-correction is a practiced response to life's ever-changing atmosphere. This proves what we put into practice produces who we really are and who we can become.

Many psychological studies show abuse breeds abuse, violence produces violence, empathy fosters empathy, and integrity advances integrity. Integrity is a disciplined response. It's something we have to force-feed ourselves to do, but once we keep forcing it, it becomes a part of our persona. It's just that simple, but it takes staying power, perseverance.

When we concentrate on integrity and honesty in our lives, we work hard to base our relationships on trust, and honesty. Mr. Rogers, during a 2002 Dartmouth commencement address, defined truth as the ultimate nourishment of our souls. He said,

> It's not the honors and the prizes, and the fancy outsides of life which ultimately nourish our souls. It's the knowing that we can be trusted. Trust is the bedrock of our lives, from which we make our choices.

Otherwise, if we emphasize manipulation and lying—the Anti-King—we build our relationships on falsehoods and dishonesty. Without integrity there cannot be trust; without trust there can be no meaningful interaction, cooperation, or interpersonal growth with family, friends, or co-workers. This is why the leading cause of divorce is lying to each other. Lying kills trust and trust is the key ingredient to all normal, productive relationships. Without trust there is no lasting relationship. This is why the Book of Truth says, "Truthful lips endure forever, but a lying tongue lasts only a moment."[23]

Even criminals must trust each other. While in Chicago as an FBI agent, I assisted in the investigation of three burglars. They were planning to burglarize a bank by burrowing into the safe deposit room from a wastewater channel directly under the bank. They were going to dig in on a Friday night of a three-day weekend, and spend the long weekend cutting into hundreds of safety deposit boxes. The FBI got wind of their devious plan and through an informant determined where they were going to hold their last meeting before the burglary. It was at a hotel where we were able to ensure they could obtain only one room. We set listening devices to record their meeting. During the meeting, the head burglar paused as we could hear the papers being unpacked and said to his three accomplices, "Now listen, we got to trust each other here, or this is never going to work." He was right, without trust his illicit deed could not have been accomplished because he needed significant truthful interaction and cooperation. "Therefore each of you must put off falsehood and speak truthfully to his neighbor . . ."[24]

The key to the King of Verbal Chess is trust. Who do we let into our confidence that we don't trust? Who will we open our heart to and communicate our inner secrets to? No one if they do not have integrity! However, most of the time not trusting is synonymous with not liking. Usually when people say they dislike somebody it's because in some way that person has lied to them, or they have seen or heard they have lied to others, and now they cannot trust them.

It is very important to understand this last truism in regard to integrity. *We will never have to apologize for having integrity. And conversely, there is no apology good enough for the lack of integrity.* Integrity is our nature's most important truism.

Self-Control, the Separate Wisdom

Self-control is sparing words, keeping an even temper, a cool spirit, and a calm center. In Verbal Chess, self-control is the wisdom to maintain our inner restraint and the calmness to enable us to deliver continual strategic responses.

"Make every effort to add to your knowledge self-control and to self-control, perseverance."[25] How old is this saying? It is biblical and was written over sixteen hundred years ago. This is significant, because it proves humans have had self-control problems since the beginning of human time. This has been my personal struggle my whole life. It has most likely also been yours.

I believe that self-control is literally and profoundly a separate wisdom. This is why we, ". . . make every effort to add to our faith goodness; and to goodness, knowledge; and to knowledge, self-control; and to self-control, perseverance." It is the freedom from yielding to the urge to do what one feels and instead doing what we should and need to do. It is the freedom of controlling choices which counter selfish impulses. This separate wisdom occurs when we have the firm realization that we are driven by two natures, the takers—those who serve their own interests and disregard others—versus the givers, who have love for others just like they love themselves (Christ's second greatest commandment[26]).

There is the old story about how every person has two wolves in them, a bad wolf, and a good wolf. Which one will they be, the good or the bad wolf? The answer is, they will be the one they feed. It is self-control which separates the two wolves. The good wolf has self-control, and the bad wolf has selfish desires. Sadly, history proves the bad wolf acts like a parasite and devours its host.

Even brilliant people are susceptible to losing their self-control . . . and their credibility. I was in a tense meeting with a large company: their CEO, three attorneys, and the human resources manager. I was presenting the results of a significant investigation. The truth was not going their way, and in the middle of my presentation one of the attorneys lost it. He stood shaking his finger at me, talking so fast he was hardly understandable. He yelled obscenities and accused my forefathers of adultery. I sat down while his verbal tirade (Anti-King warfare) was spewing from his mouth. I made no reply; I controlled my outward countenance and I just sat there giving him my undivided attention. In my heart of hearts, I wanted to stick my hand down his throat and . . . (You know the rest), but I composed myself, telling myself this too would pass. I wanted to react, but I had my company's credibility and the investigation at stake. When he ran out of verbal steam, I asked very politely if I could continue. "Yes," he said, "Go on!" I chose not to catch his verbal hardballs and throw them back, so they died in space. I could actually see his credibility leaving the room on the faces of all present. He verbally stuck the Anti-King impulse dagger of anger into his own heart, and worse, by the look on his face, he knew it. I sort of felt sorry for him and before I ended my presentation, I tried to give some of his rude dissertation credibility. Later after the meeting, the CEO called me into his office and apologized. I tried again to give the attorney some excuses for his combative conduct. The CEO said, "I appreciate your thoughts, but personally, I can see no excuse for losing self-control."

Self-control is the wisdom of an inflow enabler combined with strategic outflow. In other words, this wisdom enables us to calmly review what is being said (no matter how ugly the delivery), by separating our emotions from our impulses. This is purposefully delivering a silent or spoken response that edifies and educates the person who is playing verbal warfare. Without self-control I could not have listened and produced an immediate, controlled, edifying response. Edifying is looking for an opportunity to enlighten or bless our opponent. The Book of Truth says instead of attacking we ". . . feed your enemy if he is hungry. If he is thirsty give him something to drink and you will be 'heaping coals of fire on his head.'"[27] In other words, give an adverse opponent the opportunity to feel ashamed of himself or herself (the burning coals) for what they have done.

In order to maintain composure and restraint, we have to practice this in our everyday lives, put it into action, and fear the effect of uncontrolled responses. This practice has to be focused: self-control has to become a passion! It must become a true inner "want and must need," something that we will make a habit, a learned inner trait.

Once we are focused on this want and need "self-control," we then have to pay acute attention to our ego. I call it the "ego dance." This verbal dance is between two people who are trying to maintain ownership over an idea or thing. Arrogance is the dominate player in the ego dance. Understanding this will pave the way for pinpointing our own emotional flash points that start the verbal overflow of immediate negative responses. Verbal overflow is uncontrolled running of the mouth and is the Anti-King. Without the true development of self-control, we may instinctively go to the mind of the Anti-King, the self-justified uncontrolled anger that morphs into the next step: revenge. Neither is in the sphere of self-control, nor belongs in the game of the Christian Art of Verbal Chess.

Therefore, to maintain self-control we must have the knowledge that our personal space can be controlled by ego. Ego is the part of the mind that is responsible for reality testing. Ego can closely be tied to arrogance and can become our self-image if we are not careful, because it is not connected to reality. It then becomes the precursor to anger, the main enabler of conflict. Ego is one of the greatest barriers to effective communication.

Overcoming our ego dance with self-control is learning how to delay impulses and develop ways to keep anger from materializing—which is the key. This is impulse suppression and is a learned response. Once recognized and learned, it helps us embrace the challenges of self-control, and cope with the inevitable frustrations of life. Suppressing anger supports learning we can't control what others do, *we can only control our response.* From this we are able to detach our ego, control our anger, and see the overview of any life situation.

This overview truthfully lets us see the effect of our actions from outside our normal vision. It unveils the reasons for our own and other's behavior. Most of all this vision, or view, provides us with the first impulse of understanding instead of activating our anger. We see people's frustrating actions as a normal part of life. This realization and self-development of our "New Wisdom," begins to control our responses and moves us toward the ultimate freedom of self-control. Self-control becomes our inner trait, the freedom of choice, which we can rely on instead of no choice, which is impulse gratification. Acting from self-control will lead to self-credibility instead of self-destruction.

From my own personal experience, when I put on my investigator hat, no one can incite or upset me. I had conditioned myself in this professional realm of my life. Once, as an FBI agent, I had the pleasure of helping expel the Iranian Council out of Chicago. This was when Iran had taken over our American Embassy and was holding our Americans hostage. I can say back then there were tremendous feelings of dislike for the Iranian government and their revolutionary representatives. One night, I was in charge of guarding the Council to make sure they didn't sneak out before they were expelled. The news media was all around, and hungry. The Iranian local revolutionary leader, a guy named Raska, came out of their tenth-floor room and tried to make a scene. The hallway was narrow and crowded and he started yelling at me, waving his arms in my face, trying to provoke me. The cameras were running, the tension was high; the press was ready for an event. What did

I do? I stood there until he was done and said, "Good try, Raska, now hurry yourself back in there and pack, because tomorrow you are all leaving at 8 a.m., no matter what." I turned and walked away. Everyone was smiling except Raska. This turned out to be a non-news event, which was really good for me.

My success in this realm of life did not prepare me for teenagers. There was a time when my sixteen-year-old could pull my string and watch dad rotate almost at will. What was going on? Was I losing my self-control? No! I was quickly moving away from my self-control. I use the word *moving* because I was not, "losing my self-control" because no one loses it. The word *losing* symbolizes diminished fault, like losing our keys as a reason for being late. The word *losing* is a rationalized attempt to be a passive bystander and deflect some of the blame to happenstance. Could we ever say to someone who verbally assaulted us, "You couldn't help it because you lost your self-control?" If this is true, when people verbally and physically assault people, we should all start looking for their self-control. Can we just picture my family, after my daughter pulls my string, dad loses his self-control, and all my family is scurrying around looking under the table and around the house for dad's self-control? This is ridiculously funny! It is obvious we don't lose anything. We make a quick, conscious choice to surrender our self-control then exercise out-of-control conduct, which for most of us results in verbal abuse.

Many times we even rationalize so-and-so made me do it! People do influence us, but they don't control our minds and our responses. Researchers have found when confronted by an angry person, our heartbeat speeds up and we literally feel the anger from the other person. If somebody walked close to us right now, and started screaming and yelling, our heartbeats would rise. They also found that not only do we react to anger, but conversely when confronted by an empathetic and selfless person, our heartbeat slows down.

Researchers call this phenomenon "psychological synchrony." Psychological synchrony is being mad or glad at the same time as someone else, or sharing similar levels of heart rate, skin conductance, or other such biomarkers of arousal. This is a powerful reminder that our minds, emotions, bodies, and our physical reactions, are intimately intertwined and interdependent with those of others. Maintaining our self-control and displaying an empathetic response positively influences the person who is threatening or ignoring their self-control. Their heartbeat slows down and their anger arousal is diminished. Therefore, we can have a positive, peacemaking effect on others by maintaining our self-control.

There are people who honestly believe other people control their emotions, like anger or happiness, and their state of mind. They become self-professed victims of circumstance. They are false-reasoned out-of-control actors, where rationalization becomes reasoned volitional surrender of their self-control. This, when taken to the extreme, can be the most dangerous human trait. Most human predators in the world dwell in victimhood brought about by false reasoned rationalization. We should never forget this. And if we start to rationalize and surrender our self-control, it should set off internal alarms! Our minds should scream at us, "Caution, caution, you are about to verbally self-destruct!"

Lacking self-control personifies the Anti-King, making us defenseless against any impulse or temptation: money, eating, speaking, sex, anger, etc. Without self-control, impulses rule our actions, our minds, our words, our bodies, and our thoughts. We will not have mind, mouth, and body harmony without self-control, and cannot win life's communication game, the Christian Art of Verbal Chess. Self-control is a priceless inner trait.

I believe what the CEO said, "Personally, I can see no excuse for losing your self-control." We all must, hopefully, learn to arm ourselves with this separate wisdom!

Humility, the Spirit of Giving

Humility is the opposite of arrogance and pride. The absolute truth is, "When pride comes, then comes disgrace, but with humility comes wisdom." [28] Humility is the beginning of wisdom because it is the reality of who we are, and not an over estimation of who we think we are.

Boasting is a good example of the opposite of humility. I have read it in the Book of Truth, "As it is, you boast in your arrogant schemes. All such boasting is evil."[29] I once knew a man who was a multi-millionaire. He had several businesses and was as kind-hearted a man as I've ever seen. He was a man with one wife of over thirty years. His kids loved him, his extended family loved him, his employees loved him, and everyone who ever met him had kind things to say about him. He was a natural golfer and a gifted speaker. He spilled over with humility. About such a man I personally like boasting, but I never heard him—ever—exalt himself. As I look back, the only boasting he did was about his own weaknesses and others' strengths. Therefore, we should develop this part of the King's nature; Boast only of our own weaknesses and others' strengths, so that no one may credit us with more than they see in us or hear from us. Boasting of others' success is the humility reflection of the King of Verbal Chess.

The Mars probe took a picture some years back. The view was looking back at earth showing many planets aligned over what looked like millions of miles. The most distant point was this tiny blue planet, earth. I realized at that moment my true significance. I am an un-seeable speck on a tiny blue sphere in a vast universe.

This is a humbling experience, but what we gain is a truism, a humble heart that honors others. Once humbled, we see our significance in relationship to our real importance. This realization helps us understand we are not the best, the brightest, or the richest. It liberates us from the fear that we are the worst, the dumbest, or the poorest. Humility releases us from the self-destructive view of seeing ourselves with arrogance or, equally as bad, with low self-esteem. It lets us see others in a humble way that enables us to honor those whom we may have perceived as beneath us. This center is where we acknowledge both our strengths and our weaknesses without getting too wrapped up in either extreme.

This self-acknowledged reality lets us accept the humble truth of who we really are and live our lives with true humility.

So humility is synonymous with how we devote a ***balanced*** amount of energy inward toward self and outward toward others. Our human problem is we are all born selfish, so normally we must overcome self. When we do, we can consciously have the same compassion for others as we do for ourselves. This is a kind of courtesy given without expecting anything back. It is giving up something for someone else. It may be time, a parking place, or sharing an idea while not showing ownership. It is the realization that we can give to others more than what we have taken. Realizing how much we have taken and benefited gives us the humility needed to give back more than a full measure. This is why people who give from their hearts are full of humility. They are also highly respected. People who give from their hearts, care as much for others as for themselves. They have a special kindness about them.

All humans have pluses and minuses. This is real, and with humility we live in reality. Humility is the goodness, kindness, and courtesy that show through no matter our personality, position, stature, or wealth. It is something we can't fake for any length of time. It is who we truly are, not who we pretend to be. Truth says, "Do nothing out of selfish ambition or vain conceit, but in humility consider others better than yourselves."[30] Humility gives us the ability to show mercy, give compassion, and show understanding. Mercy, compassion, and understanding are putting others first. Humility is an inflow enabler, because people are drawn to those with humility and innately trust them. How others truly view our reflection is critically important to the success of Verbal Chess. Without the King's humility we become arrogant actors that not only prohibit communication, but also create an air of mistrust.

We obtain the King's humility by looking into ourselves and accepting how we fit in this universe; putting others first, being quick to applaud the success of others, suppressing the need for self-created admiration and cherished, exaggerated ideas about ourselves. Then, and only then, can we develop the true nature of humility!

Gratitude, the Act of Appreciation

Gratitude is also our response to the realization that we are dependent on each other. When we express gratitude by reaching out in appreciation, we are saying we need each other.

A few years ago, a client and friend of mine retrieved my credit card from a restaurant where I had accidentally left it after I paid for our lunch. He rushed back to the restaurant after I had called him about an hour after we had lunch together, retrieved the card, and immediately put the card in an envelope, put a stamp on it, and mailed it to me. This was an act of kindness. To show gratitude I quickly sent him a thank you card, before I received my credit card in the mail. I know from experience that a thank you in writing is stronger than a verbal thank you. A few days after he received the thank you card, I called to thank him again for his trouble. I wanted to be sure he knew the gratitude I felt for his act of kindness.

Gratitude is an expressed act of appreciation. It is a returned act of thankfulness for someone's act of kindness and concern. The biblical truth is we are to, "Stay alert, with your eyes wide open in gratitude."[31] This explanation encircles the meaning of gratitude. Only *thinking* kindness, concern, and appreciation does nothing, and therefore gratitude does not take place. Gratitude is an action word. We can think, "Oh gee, I should do something nice for that person who helped me." But if we don't do it, gratitude becomes a thought that births ingratitude.

The key to fulfilling gratitude is to need each other. All humans want to be needed and gratitude acknowledges that need and demonstrates we really care about others. This very fact enhances communication because we are seen as a person who cares. When we actively care about others, we are demonstrating we are the opposite of arrogant, the persona of the Anti-King. People who care experience the feeling of gratitude. Completing the circle of appreciation defines us as grateful.

During communication gratitude is a critical element because it enables the person being communicated with to not only experience our gratitude, but to give it back. Showing gratitude can be listening while asking open-ended questions to encourage more verbal representations from the person we are talking to. Gratitude is communicated to the other person by appreciating their point of view, their uniqueness, and possibly the simple recognition that they exist and are important to us. This enables them to feel as if they are being affirmed. Gratitude is an enhancer and sponsor of mutual respect.

Acceptance of Others

Verbal Chess acceptance is able to accept others with all their inconsistencies, complexities, and faults because we learn to accept ourselves with all of our inconsistencies, complexities, and faults. Is there anyone who is not inconsistent, complex, and flawed? Everyone is inconsistent, complex, and flawed because this is the standard with every human we communicate with. We should call this humanity.

Next, we must accept the inevitable inconsistencies and complexities that arise in every human relationship when two inconsistent, complex, and flawed people meet and try to communicate. This is very important given that we may be misunderstood.

Never forget, the acceptance of these realities allows us to establish a common ground of fallibility with one another, opening up unhampered communication that breeds actions of one accord and one voice, and therefore, enables others to communicate freely with us. Then we need to accept the reality of one of the most important processes in our moral and spiritual life. We have to sponsor and reflect life's unchangeable principles to be at peace with one another: fairness, integrity, honesty, trust, and the protection of human dignity.

The truth on acceptance was written over two thousand years ago: ". . . whatever other commandment there may be, (all) are summed up in this one rule: Love your neighbor as yourself."[32]

This is the absolute standard of acceptance. Make no mistake, acceptance is not tolerance. Tolerance compared to "love your neighbor as yourself" is a smokescreen that is totally unacceptable as a standard.

I realized later in life one of the keys to my success while interviewing the Indian woman in Montana. If we look at this woman, we see she was in life's fishbowl of rejection. She grew up rejected by her mother and rejected by the Crow tribe because she was Cheyenne. She was persecuted by the Crow police for the same reason. The police devalued her and thought she was involved in the killing of her husband. She was silently seething in anger. Mentally she was like a frustrated wild animal being tormented in a cage. She was looking to be affirmed by being listened to. These longings are what enabled me to communicate with her. The dialog door was opened by my truthful acceptance of her, with a large dose of humility thrown in for good measure. The hurdle I had to jump was cultural, economic, and historical. I didn't realize most of this at the time, but I projected an honest humility that was translated as a sincere acceptance, and I showed it, though in my heart of hearts I had numerous suspicions.

When I told her the short story of my life, I put us on equal footing. In other words, I treated her with compassion and acceptance which made us equal. Thankfully my suspicions were not exhibited in my actions, and the acceptance was reflected in everything else I did. I was able to succeed because my acceptance was truthful, not faked. If it had been fake, something I would have done—my body language or maybe my tone—would have shown through, and the interview would have died in space. She would have seen through me and I would have become like every other person in her miserable life.

In my experience I have found that true acceptance of others, putting others before oneself, breeds actions consistent with this attitude. When we consider others equal with ourselves, this enables a kinship of respect between two strangers, which transcends their education, cultural, and economic backgrounds. Most of all it helps transcend bad history we have with an individual or group.

Isn't this a short capsule of the persona of the King? This is purely striving to be at peace. The absolute truth written thousands of years ago says, "If it is possible, as far as it depends on you, live at peace with everyone."[33] Then we can stand on the foundation of peace and project peace through our outward demeanor with all our inconsistencies and complexities.

Years ago, when I was working for my father in our water well drilling and pump installation business, I went into his office as the foreman to complain about my worthless helper. My father asked me if my helper had one good quality. I said, "No, he doesn't." My dad looked me in the eye and said in a very terse tone, "You are the problem!" He went on to tell me that if I couldn't find something good about my helper then I was focusing only on the bad and could only see bad. He figuratively kicked me out of his office with a mission. He told me when I could objectively look at my helper, and express his good and bad points, I was to return and give him an accurate evaluation.

I went back to my truck and my helper said, "Why are you trying to fire me?" I told him that he was always dragging around and not paying attention to his work. He said no matter what he did I was always critical, which made him feel like shit. "So what did I expect him to act like?" In other words, he was acting like what I perceived he was. Was he fulfilling my perception of him? I asked him why he didn't tell me. He said I acted like I didn't care.

This confirmed it. It was then I recognized the real problem. This kid was sickly looking, had a high-pitched voice, and didn't take a bath. I didn't like him, plain and simple, and I certainly didn't accept him because I couldn't put him before myself. Therefore, I couldn't bring myself to communicate with him, and I was trying to predestine him to fail with my verbal and non-verbal communication.

How many times has this happened in the work environment or at home with our children? How many times has someone seemed to fail but in truth were feeling predestined by their superior's thought process? How many millions of dollars have been wasted on hiring new people only to make them fail because of a lack of good communication skills? Believe it or not, later this kid became a very good employee, in part because I was looking for and expressing a more positive view of him. I was truly giving him a chance to succeed through accepting him.

People who make every attempt to accept others by seeing as much good as there is to see, are perceived to have wisdom. Friendship is their calling card. Few speak condescendingly about them. They reflect decency and an undeniable concern for others. They honor others by accepting them for who they are. Acceptance works as an inflow enabler, letting us obtain the information necessary to make logical decisions about others. It is a critical inner discipline for the success of Verbal Chess.

Patience Equals Understanding

The Greek word for patience figuratively means, "Taking a long time to boil." What causes water to boil quickly? Water boils in direct proportion to the intensity of the flame. The hotter the flame, the faster the water boils.

Patience is the ability to wait or persevere without losing heart or resolve. It is the ability to withstand the intensity of the flame without letting go of our self-control. Patience is not naïve. It does not ignore bad behavior. It keeps the fire low and waits and listens. Can we possibly listen to somebody we view as angry, irrational, or just plain rude if we don't have patience? The capacity to put up with pain, troubles, difficulties, and hardships is patience that equals insight. The biblical truth says, ". . . be prepared in season and out of season; correct, rebuke and encourage—*with great patience* and careful instruction."[34]

The more patient we are, the more we absorb. The more we absorb, the more we understand. The more we understand, the better decisions we can make regarding every subject known to mankind. Patience is the key to listening, providing gratitude, hope, and acceptance. It is a willingness to put up with others, no matter how we feel about them. The wisest people I know are great listeners, because they absorb information before they speak; and this comes only through being patient.

The opposite of patience is impatience. How is this displayed? How do we reflect impatience? Do we show annoyance, irritation, edginess, or anger? It can be something as simple as looking at our watch while someone is trying to make a verbal point. It can be the expression on our face, the position of our arms, and it can be showing irritation or anger. All of these reflect our lack of patience.

Positioned at the head of the train, before kindness, courtesy, forgiveness, and mercy, is the engine of patience. From patience is birthed understanding. Understanding is the greatest psychological gift we can give another. It affirms them, warms them, and our patient reflection shines on them. We are perceived to be understanding, which is a key enabler to communication. True "Love is patient, love is kind. It does not envy, it does not boast, it is not proud."[35] Understanding then becomes the fruit of patience. It is critical to the success of the King of Verbal Chess.

Forgiveness Is Freedom

Forgiveness is literally giving up resentment and revenge. It is throwing our toxic trash away forever. It is the inner act of overcoming the animal urge of payback, the act of vengeance. Payback is a big problem because living with resentment doesn't produce joyful people. Such people personify the meaning of resentful and their whole demeanor projects it. They fail at the Christian Art of Verbal Chess because they are self-consumed with revenge. Many times, being self-consumed is feeling and living in displeasure or indignation. This causes them to become obsessed, miserable, uncertain, and unhappy.

The act of forgiveness frees us to conquer the psychological barrier of the desire for revenge and lets us gain the inner peace of forgiveness. This inner peace enables us to communicate with almost anyone, because nothing they say or do will stick to us. We won't catch the barbs of their tongue because, with God's help, we can forgive them on the spot for their foolishness.

When we understand this, we must ask ourselves what psychologically weighs us down? Could it be what others say and do? Could it be our own actions, which we are less than proud? Could it be things beyond our control? Is it our upbringing, lack of appreciation from others, being lied to, being the object of vengeance, or being treated unfairly?

Can humans be like a trash ship that gets filled up and weighed down with all the negativism surrounding us? Do we, occasionally or even daily, need to dump our trash in the deepest abyss in the ocean? The deepest is because we don't want to see it ever again. While we are thinking of dumping it, could we instead capture the words and deeds of others and instantly translate them into visualized irritation, guilt, even hate and revenge? What are we doing? We are turning trash into hazardous waste. We know we need to rid ourselves of this anvil of guilt or vengeance hanging around our necks but doing so is easier said than done.

How do we dump the trash that builds up and remove this anvil around our necks? How do we alleviate this stress and excuse ourselves and others for the wrongful deeds that have brought us to this point? In some of my training courses throughout the country, I have asked students, "How do you relieve stress?" They tell me they relieve stress by exercising, driving their convertibles with the top down, cooking, fishing, and all sorts of things. The Word of Truth offers a practical, effective solution: "Bear with each other and forgive whatever grievances you may have against one another."[36]

Normally many think of forgiveness as the act of conferring forgiveness on others. But in reality, the act of forgiveness mainly benefits us. Forgiveness is a selfish act we think of as selfless. Think about it, others we forgive may not even know we forgave them. Therefore, forgiveness releases us from what binds us. What binds us is the psychological baggage we carry around. Being selfless actually relieves us from the stress of selfish thinking, which is psychological baggage. Seeking revenge is an extremely selfish thought that binds us to another person or entity. Let's say this again so we can permanently fix this truth in our minds: being selfless and forgiving others actually relieves us from the stress of selfish thinking—vengeance, hate, and revenge—which are the lowest forms of selfish thinking, and the great ten-lane highway to self-destruction.

Likewise, forgiveness is the highest form of selfless thinking, and the greatest avenue to supporting others. George Washington, when complimenting General Nathanial Green after he had fought the battle of Guilford Courthouse against British forces led by General Cornwallis, said, "Although the honors of the field did not fall to your lot," Washington wrote, "I am convinced you deserved them." This is forgiveness and support written into one note.

While studying the psychology of violence I have found internal stress, for many, is the key enabler; and lack of self-control is the vehicle. One thing is for sure and we can mark this down: today's visualized thoughts are tomorrow's actions. Today's irritation is tomorrow's resentment. Today's anger is tomorrow's abuse. Today's hate is tomorrow's revenge. Today's guilt is tomorrow's fear. This is another way of illuminating what Jesus said, "Whatever is in your heart determines what you say," and "A good person produces good things from the treasury of a good heart, and an evil person produces evil things from the treasury of an evil heart."[37]

However, this truth—today's visualized thoughts are tomorrow's actions—is also our salvation. Why is this true? We get to control today's visualized thoughts and actions. This makes hate, anger, and guilt a matter of choice. We get to choose if we are going to "dishonor others, be self-seeking, easily angered, and keep a record of wrongs."[38] Believe this truism: hate, anger and guilt all come from keeping a record of real or perceived wrongs. All these recorded wrongs come from the history of relationships. And history doesn't go away with exercise, driving with the top down, or cooking. All these methods of relief are processes we go through to store, delay, and put these aggravations on the shelf, so we can carry on another day.

History is the enemy of peace—our toxic trash pile that builds up when we don't dump it often enough. When it builds up, people around us are aware we smell. Yes, we smell and resemble a trash pile of unforgiven stuff. Our actions and attitudes reek with the smell of our internal self-seeking frustrations focused on our record of wrongs. We start using vocabulary that signals we are victims of our own thoughts. We say things like, "I'm in a bad mood," as if a mood were a place we are assigned, rather than a thought process we permit into our minds. We can even go many steps farther down memory lane and blame our moods on someone else like, "He or she makes me mad," as if we are controlled by some outside force rather than by our own minds. How do we escape this misery? It is a simple step, but a giant step.

A friend of mine had so much resentment towards his fellow worker that he couldn't even talk to him. He was obsessed, miserable, depressed, and unhappy. He reeked with the smell of this bad relationship. He came to me and expressed his resentments. Resentments are history. After listening for an extended period, he asked me what I could recommend for him to do. He was really asking for another way to get back at this co-worker. It surprised him when I said it was simple but extremely difficult. He laughed asking, "What is simple and difficult?" I told him to forgive and forget, because to err is human and to forgive is healthy. Forgiveness is simple but forgetting is difficult.

"Forgive him? I would rather shoot him," he said.

Therein lies the problem. It is much easier to think vengeance than to think forgiveness. Forgiveness is the means of freeing a person from what binds them, to send away or wash out, or to give up all claims on the account.

Psychological studies show revenge, the lack of forgiveness, keeps our system stressed and puts out stress hormones. These stress hormones are directly related to sickness and pain. Forgiveness reduces stress and relieves pain. Complete forgiveness was first established in Jesus Christ around A.D. 30. Jesus Christ preached and practiced mercy all the way to the cross. He preached forgiveness for the betterment of our internal spirit, and science is now finding out how right He was.

All humans have done or said something we thought was not exactly right, and it went from bad to worse. We have all been wrong; we have gossiped, lied, and been horrible in some way or another. If we are in balance, we want to be righteous people who are good to others. So, we must find a way to keep struggling with ourselves and go on for our own betterment. We have to be able to forgive ourselves and redirect our efforts to try again. As we clearly see ourselves in the mirror of self-examination, we will move toward making it a habit to do what is right and honorable. This will keep building our character foundation.

Therefore, we need to keep learning from life's biggest lessons through personal failures. Without learning to overcome our failures we cannot have success in life, let alone communicate. Learning through failures strengthens our resolve because we see ourselves as a process of development. This is in contrast to a false view which we have made up by visualizing what we hope to be. This false outlook is the internal process leading to arrogance, which is the clouding of the truth. This is where we see ourselves dimly, but not face to face, developing the ability to push the blame for what we do onto others or circumstances to help escape the truth.

Self-denial can keep us from addressing our own bad behavior. This internal rationalization, at its worst, leads to a debilitating attribute that keeps us from communicating. We have all known people who believe the sun rises and sets on them, and we naturally don't want to be around them, (unless one is a groupie). If we continue to lie to ourselves, we can go the route that leads to depression or dejection. We never learn to take the internal punch for our wrong and keep going, committing to never do the offending action again. This process of continually seeing ourselves clearly keeps us in reality; and reality is where we want to dwell to be sound of mind.

When we can accomplish our truthful internal review, and at the same time strive for the betterment of our actions, then an interesting phenomenon takes place. Once we are able to forgive and strive to self-correct, we can love others as we love ourselves. We can also forgive others as we forgive ourselves, which is a true act of maturity. Therefore,

> When I was a child, I spoke as a child, I understood as a child, I thought as a child; but when I became an adult, I put away childish things.[39]

The true process of forgiving ourselves lets us see ourselves in a true light—a light that reveals a truthful assessment and a commitment to do better. This is not a rationalized assessment. It is looking in the mirror and seeing all our wrinkles not covered with makeup! Makeup is a very appropriate word because we ***make up*** excuses for ourselves. Wearing no makeup enables people who are sound of mind to have mercy on themselves and mercy on others. Mercy is both positive and negative. Positive because we receive compassion and understanding; and negative because we don't deserve it though we need it. Mercy is the pardon for past acts. This internal pardon enables us to pardon others for their wrinkles. It lets us set realistic expectations for ourselves and others. This happens when we firmly know what we or others intend is not faultless, or without error, and nothing we or others achieve is without fallibility.[40] Now we are dealing in reality, and we can then treat others with forgiveness.

Aristotle said, "We are what we repeatedly do. Excellence, therefore, is not an act . . . but a habit!" Therefore, commit this to habit: today's visualized thoughts channeled through forgiveness are tomorrow's actions. Today's irritation channeled through forgiveness is tomorrow's acceptance. Today's hate channeled through forgiveness is tomorrow's friendship. Today's anger channeled through forgiveness is tomorrow's calm. Today's guilt channeled through forgiveness is tomorrow's optimism. Forgiveness is a critical discipline in the Christian Art of Verbal Chess.

Faith and Belief in Others

There are many different quantities of faith. First, we can have faith in ourselves. Second, we can show faith in others. Third, we can have faith in what others are capable of doing. "Faith is the assurance of things hoped for and the conviction of things not seen."[41] Faith is recognizing something that is already a reality despite the fact that it cannot be seen. Faith in ourselves cannot be seen but gives us confidence that if we work hard, we will see the result. Faith in others encourages them to have faith in themselves. The sense of being valued gives them the confidence that they can do it. This is the assurance of things hoped for. The giver of faith knows this is a reality, but the receiver cannot see, touch, or feel it—but knows it is real. It is the tangible and real proof of what we know to be true but cannot see. There is true power in giving faith because it transcends into a person's belief in his or herself.

However, some people think that whatever they want they can simply imagine into existence. This makes faith in others much more complicated. We know faith has no creative power, so others cannot make it up. Faith in others only comes through questioning and testing. Since all people are inconsistent, complex, and flawed we must question and test them to have faith in them. Therefore, if we're going to have faith in others, we have to be able to question the things they do and test their reliability.

A questioning attitude says, show me first because most people have a hard time faking goodness for any length of time and over 90% of people lie. So, when I'm confronted with a choice of trusting or not, I'm not going to say I do not trust someone, but I'm *not* going to take everything they say as fact either. The Book of Truth reveals the reason for questioning:

> Only a simpleton believes everything he's told! A prudent
> man understands the need for proof.[42]

We must have a questioning attitude and a period of evidence-based testing to have legitimate faith in others. Unlike animals, people can have a multitude of different faces. They can trick, con, lie, manipulate, and coerce others, even while being a deacon in a local church. Humans are multifaceted in nature. And because humans can portray themselves as many different people, faith testing is very hard to do but must be done.

For example, as an FBI agent I interviewed a man who was a killer. He lived a life of portraying himself as good when he was evil. He was truly a psychopath but had the outward countenance of a kind and engaging person. He told me I didn't have to fear him because deep down in his soul he was a kind man. He even had the audacity to motion with his hands that I could unhandcuff him. Did I have any faith in him? He later admitted to killing eight people and then told me with the ease of a man who was doing something nice that all of them would have thanked him.

Dealing with others with a questioning attitude enables us to grow self-confidence and a confirmed conviction that we are able to feel or perceive things even though they are not seen. I could feel the evil from the man above. My skin tingled and my palms were sweating. I was having a very hard time not showing I was aghast. This is being able to understand others at a higher level of discernment. It is when all our senses are working overtime.

We must first develop faith in ourselves, or we'll have a really hard time developing faith in others, or faith in the intangible realities like patience, hope, gratitude, and forgiveness. Instead, we will constantly question ourselves. We must be willing to climb the mountain of doubt in order to reach the height of belief. This brings us to faith in what we have discovered. Therefore, developing faith in others starts with doubt, then discovery through questioning and testing to confirm belief or disbelief, which then determines the amount of faith we will put in others.

Then how is faith projected from us? All we have to do is look at how we deal with our children. My daughters used to play a game of gymnastics and when they would finally be able to accomplish a move, like a somersault, they would want me and my wife to watch. In watching with our undivided attention, we would give belief and faith, and they would receive joy for their accomplishment. What if they messed up? Then we would give encouragement (belief) and express faith that they could do it.

Through these faith-filled positive actions, something stronger takes place. When we project faith during subtle interactions—a positive tone of voice, facial expression, touch, or posture—we communicate our expectations to others. Such faith-filled communication helps others by supporting their positive perception of themselves, enabling them to see themselves in a better light, or with greater potential. They internalize our belief in them, and they are able to transcend their internal doubts to believing they can do it. Even if we merely create the idea in their minds that the task is possible, we are enabling them to succeed. This is not a control process; it is giving others the faith they need to succeed. It does not ensure success, but it creates the avenue for success.

Telling people they can do something difficult, and then supporting them with belief through their temporary failures, gives them the strength to reach impossible dreams beyond self-imposed limitations. We are telling others they are worth our undivided attention and through belief we have unfailing faith in them. They are worth our time, and most of all they are receiving our faith in their future actions. This faith proves to their inner fears, no matter what, they have someone who will not give up on them. This is where we know "If you do not stand firm in your faith, you will not stand at all."[43] Herein lies the strength and support to enable others to change their perception of what they can and cannot do. They have someone who believes in them and this opens every avenue of communication.

When I was a junior in high school, we were in a football game with our rival school. It was the first time I ever played running back, and we were leading fourteen to nothing. I had run for ninety plus yards in the first half and scored both touchdowns and the extra points. The coaches were discussing the strategy for the second half, when one coach said we should stop running and start passing, because all we did in the first half was run. Now, I've never been what anyone would call a running back, because previously I was the center. The center is the one who hands the ball to the quarterback. Then he blocks the defensive guard or linebacker.

The team was practicing a few days before this game against our rivals. The big guy who was the running back was really messing up. He couldn't seem to find the hole we would make and kept running right up my back. It was rumored that he closed his eyes when he got the ball. I finally got pissed and ripped off his helmet and yelled a few cuss words, loudly explaining that anyone could run through the hole our offensive line had made for him. Well, the coach decided to give me a try and guess what? This slow-moving, 156 lb. kid didn't do that bad in practice. But we all know there is a world of difference between practice and the game. And, at that point in the game, I sure had my doubts.

During the actual game, the other team, toward the end of the half, started yelling my number before the ball was handed to me and I was getting punished pretty badly. My lip was bleeding, my back was sore. Back then we had only one bar on the helmet to protect our faces, and the other team was punching me in the face. Truthfully, I was kind of agreeing with the coach who said to pass more, but then it happened.

In the locker room at halftime the head coach shook his head, and said to the other two coaches, "I believe Howard can do it." The three coaches looked at me, and one said, "Can you keep pounding away?"

"Yes," I said. We all gathered around the coach and said a prayer. We could do that back then because we knew there was a Higher Power, and we started for the door. The head coach grabbed me and looked me in the eye, and nodded in a knowing way and said, "You can do it!"

"You bet, Coach," I said. And if the coach said I could do it, I could do it. Out the door I ran to my last football game. Last because the next year I got hurt and couldn't play, but like I said, I was no real running back anyway. I was slow and wore the high-top shoes of a lineman. As a lineman, I knew where the holes were going to be in the offensive line the linemen would create. Most of all in the second half of this game, I had the coach's faith in me. I ran for over seventy-five yards in the second half and scored one more touchdown and another extra point. We won twenty-one to nothing. It is interesting, I don't remember the coach's name, but I will never forget the faith he had in me.

Faith can move mountains![44] Faith is paradoxical because it goes beyond reason and has two sides. One side has to do with the intellect and the other has to do with will. Faith in a higher being—God, for example—involves intellect, belief, and faith, not necessary in that order.

Numerous studies have shown that those of us who believe in a higher being, such as Christians and Jewish people, have a greater will to be effective humans. We have a moral standard to live by. We have faith, the assurance of things hoped for, and the intellectual conviction of things not seen. This goes beyond the normal reasoning power of humans. Having faith in Christ enables us to trust in God, and through this faith we have the knowledge that God sees us as sons and daughters. This is a powerful spiritual support in the believer's life. I recommend to all that we dive deep into faith in God and cultivate this faith by using our intellect and will power. This will build in us the assurance of things hoped for and the conviction of things not seen. It is at the very least a tremendous psychological stabilizer in a person's life.

Once faith is bestowed on us, we can believe in ourselves. This strengthens us beyond recognition. Recognition came after the game when I received a game ball. The recognition, although good, is past based; faith is future based. It doesn't have to be conveyed through a special presentation or event, it can be projected simply through our countenance. Like my coach grabbing my jersey and looking me in the eye with confidence. Faith builds confidence, not arrogance. Faith builds strength of character, not deception. Communicating this truth to your kids, spouse, friends, employees, students, and everyone around us will become an intervening medium, through which our faith in others will enable them to grow to be effective humans.

Can our positive words and countenance, combined with faith in others, change a person's life in a positive way that could last a lifetime? Yes, faith can and we can! "I have faith in you," is one of the most powerful truths we can learn. Faith is a key enabler to productive communication.

Hope and Perseverance

Hope is a cherished desire with anticipation of obtaining fulfillment. Perseverance is the continued effort to achieve something despite difficulties. When these two characteristics combine, they form an unbeatable discipline.

This is written in the Book of Truth,

> For in hope we have been saved, but hope is not what we see, for that is not hope. We hope for what we do not

see, because _hope_ gives us the <u>perseverance</u> to conquer the unknown.[45]

To understand hope, we must understand the uniqueness of hope and how it is the very essence of perseverance. When I was in the Army in Korea, I came across a GI who was in the hospital recuperating from injuries received in Vietnam, and we became quick friends. After a period of weeks Tim related this story of hope and perseverance to me.

Neither he nor I totally understood at the time that this event was related to hope, but in this story is a deep, undying hope in the God Tim didn't even know he had. This hope enabled him to keep going, to have perseverance. I'll try to do the story justice.

Tim was guarding a bridge with about a hundred other GIs north of Saigon when in the early morning of January 31, 1968, the Tet Offensive started, during which seventy thousand North Vietnamese Army and Viet Cong guerrillas launched surprise attacks throughout Vietnam at more than one hundred cities and outposts. This was his outpost.

When it started Tim was half sleeping while sitting slumped against three layers of sandbags in front of a line of foxholes protecting a main bridge. _Half sleeping_ because he said, "You never really sleep at night in war." Flares started going off and claymores (a kind of landmine) exploded waking him from his stupor. The claymores were trip-wired in front of their location. He looked over the sandbags towards the village and heard the sound of bugles blaring. He could see through the light of their flares what seemed like hundreds of black outlined bodies with blinking lights in front of them. From a slight rise to the right front of the attack came green tracers which at first were going over their heads, and then they could hear the heavy bullets striking their sandbagged position.

The Vietnamese (VC) must have snuck into the village under cover of darkness because they were running at them from that direction. The blinking lights were flashes of fire from their rifles. The green tracers were 51-caliber Russian machinegun bullets. Tim could hear heavy impacts against the outer sandbags, and then sand stung his face as the heavy bullets exploded into the bags next to his face. He got down, face stinging, heart pounding, thanking God they had put PSP (perforated steel plate) in the middle of the sandbags. He started fumbling with his M-16 making sure the safety was off, not wanting to rise.

The sergeant yelled to start firing. Tim forced himself to rise, somehow keeping his urge to run under control, using every ounce of self-discipline to control his fear. Later he would say, "The bravest thing I ever did in Viet Nam was raise up over those sandbags and fire back." He fired directly at several of the flashes and to his surprise, they stopped. He could not see well enough to tell exactly what he was hitting. He dropped down trying to figure out why his M-16 had stopped firing and discovered he had emptied the twenty-round magazine. He reloaded, putting in another magazine, telling himself to take it easy. He rose when something popped like a watermelon beside him; he turned his head not understanding what the wetness was which was hitting him in the face. At the same moment, a guy called Pop who was standing next to him, flew backwards. Tim stooped low, looking back. Half of Pop's head was missing. He turned facing the sandbags, not feeling any physical pain—just the psychological pain from the instant inner agony over Pop's death. He was stunned for a second; using his left sleeve he wiped Pop's blood out of his left eye, trying to get the courage to rise again. His mind seemed cloudy with the overwhelming, momentary thought of how much Pop wanted to live. He, as if he were looking from the outside, could see his body mechanically moving, moving to direct the aim of his rifle to fire. His determination was building as he fired, and more flashes stopped with dark bodies falling. This he realized was a battle of individual determination. Each GI behind those sandbags was feeling the same pain of fear as the VC who were forging ahead like Picket's Charge during the Civil War. They all knew the ones with the greatest perseverance and firepower would win.

He stooped again, reloaded, noticing the lieutenant crouching to his right was yelling into the radio mic trying to get fire support. He rose, firing. Now some of the VC were within fifty yards, and every one of the GIs was firing his M-16 on full automatic. To his left, their Quad 50 machineguns on a Deuce-and-a-Half Truck suddenly opened up; he realized it had not been firing. He learned later a sniper killed the first gunner the moment the initial claymores went off.

Tim was firing as fast as he could aim. He was yelling at the top of his voice, but with the sound of hundreds of rifles, machineguns, and the Quad 50—not to mention the North Vietnamese rifles, rockets, and mortar explosions—he couldn't hear anything. He was heartened the Quad 50 with four .50 caliber machineguns were really wiping them out. "Those guns are death machines," he thought quickly.

The VC charge slowed with the Quad 50 mowing them down. He could see the flashes stop in bunches as the Quad 50 fired five-second bursts. The VC small arms fire started to die, but their mortar rounds immediately picked up the pace and started coming in fast.

"Damn," he said to himself, "they know what they're doing!"

The VC were trying to knock out the Quad 50. It was the heaviest weapon the GIs had. It was their barrier from annihilation without further fire support.

The lieutenant yelled, "Incoming!" The soldiers slowed their fire as they heard the sounds of the mortar explosions. Wham! The high explosive mortar round landed several yards behind Tim. The concussion knocked him off his feet, but he wasn't hurt. One second, two seconds, three seconds, Tim was scrambling to get up, then wham, another mortar round exploded. Then faster, wham, wham, as multiple mortar rounds went off over and over. They were now landing all around the GIs' position on the north end of the bridge. Quickly glancing back, he could see the south end of the bridge through the light of the flares. The GIs on the south end were safely hunkered down watching the mortar flashes. Tim felt envious.

"We have no mortars!" he said aloud. All they could do was put their heads and bodies in their holes. He heard GIs yelling, "Medic, medic!"

"We're being killed!" He yelled the obvious, feeling helpless. Then the bugles started again. "They're coming again," yelled the sergeant. The mortar rounds didn't stop: wham, wham, wham!

"I can't live through this," he thought to himself, not knowing whether to rise to fight and die, or to stay in his hole and die. He was quickly standing, firing, and yelling. A big explosion erupted off to his left. He dropped, crouching, trying to protect himself, and looked at the Deuce-and-a-Half. Fire was coming out of the top of the truck. The sergeant yelled the obvious, "They got the Quad 50!"

Being only human, he thought it was all over. He got calm all of a sudden; it was as if the sound of terror went away. Everything was moving, firing, and exploding, but now the sound and fear didn't bother him. He had mentally moved into that other world where only those warriors go who can control their fear (and few get back). This world is where the chances of survival are dim, but determination creates hope. Tim started repeating a biblical Scripture over and over; he did not remember where it came from. It went something like this, ". . . glory to God . . . produces perseverance; and perseverance, character, and hope." Tim slowed down and was somehow comforted as he took methodical aim. With every single shot a blinking light stopped. Now he was in a place where nothing mattered except survival and survival meant placing the bullet where it would kill and kill.

He felt as if he were outside his body looking in. He said to himself, "If I'm going to die, I'm going to kill as many as I can. Didn't I hear that in an old western?" He chuckled and immediately could not believe he could say Scripture, laugh, and kill at the same time. He was past determination, past fear. He was killing to survive, killing to stop the predator of death. It was his only hope, and somehow, he knew Christ was with him. He dropped to reload, and heard his lieutenant, with the microphone to his mouth, "Red Leader, this is Touchdown. White flares mark our position. Lay it fifty yards north of the white flares."

There was too much noise for him to hear the reply. "Negative, Red Leader! North of the white flares! Red Leader, Red Leader—%&@!" the lieutenant yelled, "He's going to kill us."

A flight of Phantom jets were circling to provide fire support until Puff the Magic Dragon could get there, but apparently the lieutenant thought the Phantoms were screwed up on exactly where they were. The pilots looked down on a battle in the middle of the night, with no moon. It had to be confusing, he thought, in between firing and loading.

"Their radio must not be working right," he thought. He heard the lieutenant yell again, "North of the white flares. The white flares mark our position. (Pause) No, you dumb %&@!, north, north!"

They were coming. He could hear the Phantom jets and knew they would use their Vulcan 20mm Gatling gun. The gun could shoot six thousand rounds per minute, one hundred rounds a second of tracer, armor-piercing, and high explosive incendiary (HEI) rounds in an astonishing killing package. Nothing lived where those rounds landed. The tracers tell the pilots where they are hitting, the armor piercing goes through everything, and the HEI rounds explode and burn what is left. "God," he thought to himself, "I'm going to die!"

The lieutenant ducked, thinking his own planes were going to kill him. Tim turned in a crouch, fell back against the sandbags, waited for his death, and stared into the sky looking south. Hope faded into a memory, and death was expected.

"%&@!," he said to himself, "either way I'm going to die; what does it matter?" It's peculiar, he thought, how when you finally know the end is near what a relief you feel, but at the same moment he felt guilty. He felt no pain, his face didn't sting, and he felt strangely clean. He didn't feel any sticky blood on his face from Pop's head. He relaxed and gave in, saying to himself with regret, "After all, I don't want to die all tensed up. God, I'm ready!"

The red tracers looked like they were coming right at them, but in a flash, over them. The sound of the 20mm Gatling gun roaring over the sound of the jets was like saying the word *was*, leaving off the *s*: WAAAAAAAAAA. The ground exploded around the VC just a few yards in front of their sandbags. Three more

Phantoms came in and laid it down the same way: WAAAAAAAA, then WAAAAAAAAAA, and another WAAAAAAAAAA.

"Kill the %&@!ers!" He was trying to yell as he raised himself from certain death, only no sound was coming out. He had lost his voice. Tim continued to rise, elated to be alive, peering over the bags and thanking God. The ground had turned white where the VC had been because of the HEI rounds. "Where did they go?" he said to himself.

The lieutenant said, "Those %&@!ers did it. Oooh, %&@! I thought I was dead!" to no one in particular.

Tim stooped over, half realizing he was back from that other world and among the living. He could feel his heart pumping again. He collapsed in his hole, feeling totally worn out, but happy to be alive.

The lieutenant yelled into the mic, "You %&@!ers did it!"

It got strangely quiet, and he was able to hear the flight leader say, "This is dumb %&@!. We are glad you're alive."

"Red Leader, sorry about that. It was pretty bad down here," the lieutenant said.

"Roger, Touchdown," the pilot said. The lieutenant nodded to no one and put the mic down before leaning against the sandbags, exhausted.

This story shows the extremes of life and death, and how in the midst of hell, the ability to have hope gives us the tenacity to carry on under the most extreme conditions. Tim had hope until the moment he was convinced the jets were going to kill him; then he had peace. Upon realizing the jets had done the opposite, hope was rewarded, and he lived again.

Three more times the VC came back that night, and three more times the GIs repulsed an enemy force many times greater than their own. Tim told me that as long he repeated the Scripture (he later found out it was Romans 5:3-5) he felt he had hope. "Christ's hope," he said, "made me fight harder by giving me perseverance. Hope combined with Christ is so powerful that without hope I felt doomed." He summarized saying, "Hope comes first, then determination, tenacity, and staying power, which equal perseverance."

Hope in Christ provides us with the inner commitment to keep putting one foot in front of the other. We develop a hopeful attitude through effort, discipline, patience, and concentration. Hope is not believing that everything will turn out alright, rather, it is the conviction that even when things go wrong, somehow, we will find a way to make it through. Hope provides us with the inner commitment to keep putting one foot in front of the other. That's how we learn it. We develop a hopeful attitude in learning how to believe in ourselves and believe in others. Hope is conveyed in both our attitude, "I can do it," and our actions, "I will do it."

The truth is the Christian Art Verbal Chess hope is tenacious. It is like the old song, "I get knocked down, but I get up again. You are never gonna keep me down."[46] Researchers have confirmed through numerous studies that hope has a deep and lasting impact on our minds, bodies, and spirits. Hope, according to these studies, strengthens our relationships, enhances creativity, calms us down, improves work performance, and helps us refuse to give up! Hope is an enabler to communication, and we are healthy and sound of mind when our persona is filled with hope. This is just the kind of person we like to communicate with—a positive, always-seeing-the-bright-side kind of person. Hope becomes part of our reflection and is highly contagious. It spreads to others and inspires confidence in others. Hope is a most important inner discipline that will positively affect others.

The question is: where is the right path and how do we find it? How do we know integrity, self-control, humility, gratitude, acceptance, patience, forgiveness, faith, and hope, with an abundance of perseverance, are the right ingredients?-

To discover how we are living, read what is revealed in the Book of Truth.

> Even so, every good tree bears good fruit, but a bad tree bears bad fruit. A good tree cannot bear bad fruit, nor can a bad tree bear good fruit. Every tree that does not bear good fruit is cut down and thrown into the fire. Therefore by their fruits you will know them.[47]

> For it is by grace you have been saved, through faith—and this is not from yourselves, it is the gift of God . . .[48]

The Nature of the King

To build our foundation of communication on the unchangeable principles of life we must focus on being the nature of the King of Verbal Chess. This is developed through maturing our nature, and this change is always produced in elemental stages. First, the intellectual element is the change of mind. Second, the emotional element is the change of heart. Third, the volitional element is the change of will. All three, mind, heart, and will are what change our nature. In other words, we visualize the benefit through our mind (intellect), and feel through our heart (emotional), that we have to change; and then we affect the change when we will (volitional) it to be changed. The change of mind affects the heart, and the change of heart enables us to have the will to change our lives.

This process is what I call true wisdom because wisdom comes from learning, watching others, and recognizing our own failures. Learning from our own failures and those of others starts in the mind, flows through the heart, and lets our will affect the change in our own performance. This process is an uncommon wisdom. The Christian Art of Verbal Chess King is filled with this wisdom, the wisdom of volitional enhancement. This "wisdom that is from above is first pure, then peaceable, gentle, willing to yield, full of mercy and good fruits, without partiality and without hypocrisy."[49]

Conclusion

A true example of the Anti-King is revealed in the story of King Hezekiah who, "was too proud to show gratitude for what the Lord had done for him," and his people suffered. Arrogant people, on different levels, do not care about others; they give themselves credit. They operate in the fishbowl of the selfish mind, do not show genuine gratitude, and do not enhance communication because communication to them is a means to get what they want.

When we live within the Anti-King mentality, we are forever destroying bridges that are necessary to pass over and return during our lives. These destroyed bridges are the virtues of the King of Verbal Chess; integrity, self-control, humility, gratitude, acceptance, patience, forgiveness, faith, and hope, that gives us perseverance. In reality, when the Anti-king destroys these bridges, they are destroying friends, family, and associates—the most important people in our lives to honor and respect.

The King of Verbal Chess, you may have discovered, is the character of Christ, the King of all Kings.[50] We have all heard honesty is the best policy, well, it is more than just honesty. It is loving your neighbor as yourself. It is our motives that naturally look out for the best interests of others. It is a kindness and humbleness that is legitimate and self-controlled so when life's challenges hit, when we least expect it, we can overcome ourselves and be the person Christ wants us to be. The King of Verbal Chess is our goal. It is the royalty of the Christian Art of Verbal Chess because when we strive to emulate the King, we make our lives closer to being like Christ. The closer we get to this goal, the more others will feel inclined to honor and respect us and this enables us "speak life into others".

5

The Queen

THE SKILL OF GIVING GRACE

AS WE HAVE looked at the chessboard, we have described the King and our opposition the Anti-King (which can be ourselves or our opponent). The King is the most important part because if we lose the traits he represents, we have lost the game of Verbal Chess. However, the King cannot secure victory on his own. He needs the help of the rest of the pieces on the board. The most powerful ally on his side is the Queen; and his most powerful opposition is the anti-Queen.

The Queen is our most versatile piece and the most difficult to learn. It works from within every piece on the Verbal Chess side of the playing field. The Queen can move multiple spaces forward, backward, and diagonally with ease. In the game of Verbal Chess, the Queen represents the skill of grace. The Queen has the power to impartially step into another's life, see the world through their eyes, and selflessly give mercy and compassion to gain insight. At the same time the Queen is able to step back and see the reality of the situation. The Queen is truly our spirit of the game, the art of graciousness. "Let your conversation be gracious and attractive so that you will have the right response for everyone."[51]

Finding a way to influence others in a positive way should be the goal of every manager, parent, and pastor—every person.

And certainly, all of us should desire to positively influence our spouses, friends, family, and especially our children. The Queen is the act of giving grace accomplished by vicariously experiencing the feelings, and thoughts of others. The Queen of Verbal Chess is the spiritual key to all successful communication.

Remember the story about when I couldn't find the good in my helper? What did it take? Remember the Indian woman? What gives us the opportunity to connect with people transcending culture, background, and biases? The Book of Truth gives us the answer by stating, ". . . since you excel in faith, in speech, in knowledge, in all diligence, and in your love for others—see that you abound in this grace."[52]

Giving grace is the essence of a sports story, which concludes with the player talking about his coach. "He has a knack for finding the good in everybody. That's easier said than done. Not everybody can find the good. But once he finds that good, he just focuses in on the good. And finding the good automatically weeds out the negative. He does this for everybody on the team. It makes you want to go out and give him your all."

Many company executives today say they are having a hard time developing employees who will give their all to their jobs. They create systems to weed out bad employees instead of developing them, because frankly most do not know how to communicate with unproductive workers. Therefore, they try to find the one good producer in the patch of weeds. We can hardly blame them.

Parents have the same difficulty with unproductive, self-serving children. Parents try to impose rules. Some even put their children down, or get mad and call them names, or tell them they are lazy, rather than trying to positively motivate them. Even pastors have the same difficulty with parishioners who are difficult and uncooperative. Also, there are co-workers who are disdainful to talk to and make everyone around them miserable. These are the people in the world who dwell in the land of the Anti-King, and they desperately need someone to give them compassion and mercy.

Many of these people today are the way they are because they do not have the benefit of an upbringing in a functional family with a mother and father. In the inner cities today, it has been reported ninety-three percent of children are born in fatherless homes. It is foolish to wonder what is wrong when our culture is ignoring the bedrock of society, the family. The Book of Truth says parents "... must manage their own family well and see that their children obey them, and they must do so in a manner worthy of full respect."[53] This assumes there is a father and a mother.

Therefore, because of their upbringing, countless people today have not learned the skill of being graceful with others in their communication. They never obtained the core values necessary for a productive and honorable life that can come from a functional family with a mother and father. There is a direct correlation between learning the skill of giving grace and learning from our mistakes. Succeeding is making adjustments; but failure is quitting. Successful communication is founded on learning from our mistakes and giving grace to ourselves and others, because all humans are inconsistent, complex, and flawed.

Many people today seem to have forgotten when humans fail to learn to overcome failures, they cannot learn how to succeed. Let me repeat this: without learning to overcome failure, humans cannot learn how to succeed. This is how we learn to use the Queen of Verbal Chess. A great example is the story of Thomas Edison who failed more than one thousand times when trying to create the light bulb. When asked about it, Edison said, "I have not failed one thousand times. I have successfully discovered one thousand ways to NOT make a light bulb." I'm thankful Thomas Edison did not go to school today or we might still be using candles.

There have been numerous studies on the subject of overcoming failure and becoming successful. The point here is learning to give grace, the Queen of Verbal Chess, will challenge us. Experiencing difficulties and overcoming communication failures are part of the necessary maturing process critical to the development of humans who thrive and flourish in all facets of the game of life, communication. Without learning to overcome failure, people can become self-serving failures, and never see themselves as the problem. They believe themselves to be entitled, leading them to think the fault lies anywhere other than with themselves. They unconsciously buy into the circle of failure, making the same mistakes, over and over, thinking they are going to have a different result. Albert Einstein called this insanity.-

To thrive in this life is to prosper in communication. To prosper in communication requires the acknowledgment that we will fail at times. Learning to study and work hard is learning to overcome and to never give up. This is the epitome of competition: the awareness we may win or lose, but no matter what, we will always rise to compete again. We learn we "reap what we sow." In communication this can be gained through connecting with people in a special way; but this special way is a mystery to some in this microwave world where everything has to be done in less than three minutes.

"So, how do we learn to extend grace in our communication? How do we make a connection with others that transcends our differences in culture and backgrounds and overcomes our biases?"

The Queen: The Skill of Giving Grace

Let me relate a simple situation where the lack of giving grace failed to generate a clear understanding and action. I was sitting around a lunch table with four men who were friends. One of the men said out of the blue that he would really like to see the Monday Night Football game. Some of the men looked at him with an expression like, *why is he saying that?* The conversation continued and all, including myself, were contributing and wanting to be heard. Once again, the man changed the subject and said he would really like to see the Monday Night Football game. Again, no one said anything, and the conversation drifted off to something else. I saw the look of disappointment on his face while he displayed one of those *oh well* looks. Was anyone listening? Yes, we all heard what he said. Was there any attempt to understand? No, we all felt puzzled by his statement, but no inquiry was made. Was this man given unmerited favor? No, we just continued.

Later, as we walked outside alone, I asked him what he meant, and he said he had just moved into his new home, didn't have the television hooked up, and was dreading going to a bar to watch Monday Night Football. I invited him over and was able to develop a lasting relationship. He later told me my understanding and kind action was deeply appreciated. All I did was care enough to give him (grace) compassion and mercy to try to understand and act on my insight.

I was reading the bestselling book of all time, and a sentence stood out:

> When I was a child, I talked like a child; I thought like a child, I reasoned like a child. When I became an adult, I did away with childish things. Now we see but a poor reflection in a mirror but in the future we shall see face to face. Now I know in part, but then I shall know just as I also am known. [54]

When communicating, the men sitting around the lunch table, and most of the rest of us, reflect the attitude of a child. We see ourselves like a poor reflection in a mirror when it comes to vicariously experiencing the feelings and thoughts of others. What were they missing? Grace comes from our inner predisposition of compassion, an instance of kindness and courtesy, all wrapped around giving unmerited favor. The Book of Truth says, ". . . the word of his grace . . . can build you up and give you an inheritance among all those who are blessed."[55] The unmerited favor is "being wise, and bearing with others gladly."[56] This skill comes from our internal motive of giving grace which we project as we communicate with others.

The person giving grace is giving a gift of graciousness or unmerited favor to someone in need. The giver is a sower of courteous goodwill; but a hoarder is selfish and demeans. The truth is all of us need mercy and compassion sown into us as we communicate because we, as I said previously, are all inconsistent, complex, and flawed. The Book of Truth says, "multiply your seed for sowing [that is, your resources] and increase the harvest of your righteousness [which shows itself in active goodness, kindness, and love]."[57] Sowing mercy and compassion—grace—jumps the barrier of unproductive communication by giving favor, which gives joy and creates an atmosphere of freedom to express our inner-most feelings.

This enables the persona of the King of Verbal Chess to be viewed as trustworthy, merciful, accessible, and friendly. The two parties communicating can even have a strained relationship and the one who shows graciousness enables the relationship to heal and reconcile because forgiveness is possible. When we create an atmosphere of giving grace, this gives us the chance of renewing failed relationships because we are creating an atmosphere of equable temperament where all relationships prosper. This is why the Queen becomes our most versatile piece on the playing field. The Queen is the virtuous spirit within the game of Verbal Chess and the spirit that works from within every piece on the Verbal Chess side of the playing field: the King, Bishop, Knight, Castle, and all the Pawns.

The Queen of Verbal Chess, as we have stated, becomes our power to impartially step into someone else's life, seeing the world through their eyes, selflessly giving mercy and compassion to gain understanding. At the same time, we are able to step back and see reality. Then we can act on the verbal and bodily information communicated by our opponent and answer in a positive and edifying way. This reveals the truth, "Let your conversation be always full of grace, seasoned with salt, so that you may know how to answer everyone."[58]

The Queen's Action Steps to Exhibit Grace

There are four combined steps to giving the Queen's grace: one, mentally stepping in; two, giving mercy and compassion to gain understanding; three, stepping back to see reality; and four, peacemaking responses and actions. Note the four steps of giving the Queen's grace are combined with each other as we gain a special kind of understanding with the added strength of the King's character. This concept is very important to comprehend because it is an avenue to understanding others.

Utilizing the Queen's grace is learning to impartially step into another's life wearing their leg braces. This is the highest order of empathy. It is called grace. It is the art of vicariously experiencing the feelings, thoughts, and attitudes of another, by using our five senses—sight, hearing, smell, taste, and touch—thereby conveying understanding.

Sight enables us to see every minute movement in the face, hands, body, and feet. Hearing is critical because of tone, rhythm, and pitch. Smell can reveal clues such as stress, occupation, nationality, activity, etc. Taste can reveal our own stress level, dry mouth etc. Touch connects us to the feelings of another in a revealing and telling way. Our senses enable us to experience and interpret the feelings of another while giving grace. Remember the Indian woman? Sight, smell, and taste enabled me to be successful in giving her grace.

When all five senses are combined with the motive of grace, we generate the sixth sense: understanding. The sixth sense is our interpretational sense or focused awareness which recognizes in others weariness, apprehension, love, joy, hate, evil, aggression, distress, sorrow, and desires. Through the process of learning to give grace, we are able to mentally and physically see through another's eyes, gaining insight, recognizing another's inner most feelings, and understanding them as much as is humanly possible. Using all our senses to develop this interpretational sense is critical during meaningful, stressful, and threatening situations. Giving grace not only enables us to interpret the present, it also may allow us to detect, through our senses, the unfolding of events before they happen.

Another step in developing the attribute of the Queen's grace is to gain awareness by showing mercy and compassion. Mercy, of course, is unmerited favor. Therefore, to selflessly give grace takes mercy focused on awareness to gain insight. All of us can have this interpretational sense, but we must thirst for this exceptional insight by giving mercy and forgiveness.

The Queen: The Skill of Giving Grace

Most men have lost our ability because we don't normally use our senses to gain understanding. Actually, we are like the old *Drag Net* TV series, "Just give me the facts." Learning to be able to mentally and tangibly step into another's life is necessary to becoming capable of recognizing another's inner-most feelings. This is a little like taking a vacation in the woods. It takes a while to start smelling the wonderful smells of the trees and plants. Once we start learning to smell—literally, all over again—everything smells better. The morning coffee smells better, and bacon, oh, how wonderful that bacon smells when camping in the mountains!

Our ability to smell or to understand is normally impaired until we start to learn to use our senses all over again. There was this saying posted in my workout gym: "If we don't use it, we lose it!" Well, we may have become sluggish because, in today's world, we have been taught to find everything quickly on our smart phones. However, a smart phone is not smart enough to gain understanding of others. Therefore, we need to realize if we don't practice using all our senses, our ability to use them and gain this interpretational sense, will be impaired.

There is hope. We get to practice communication almost every waking moment. We can easily gain the use of all our senses by forcing ourselves to give others our total attention. Total attention is simply the process of using all our senses to gain understanding of the deep mysteries of another. These deep mysteries can be understood by impartially stepping into another's life and seeing their problems. Best of all, when we start practicing the spirit of the Queen, it becomes contagious and exciting. We might even start repairing old relationships because we will start to truly understand and appreciate others.

However, some view this process as dangerous to self because it is freely giving of ourselves, both mentally and tangibly, to the process of empathetic interpretation. Most humans innately believe they are exposing themselves to vulnerabilities and are reluctant. Focusing on our vulnerabilities is a self-centered misrepresentation of the facts, a kind of fear. Fear is false evidence that appears real. This could be the fear of rejection, being exposed, verbally attacked, or losing the verbal tug of war.

The Queen's grace does not leave us vulnerable, as we will learn; we don't have to fear the results. It connects us with people in a special, deep, and insightful way that cannot be denied.

Several things can get in the way of us extending mercy and compassion to others to gain understanding. One of these is our own personal interests, or "self-concern." In other words, this is the process of not being able to get over ourselves. Self-concern is the main obstacle to gaining this valuable and satisfying connection. An overabundance of self-concern is arrogance. The key to the Queen of Verbal Chess is selflessly giving. Selflessness is being ready and willing to go to great lengths to understand. It is giving our time and attention. It is being focused and ready to take on the responsibility of understanding. Yes, part of selfless giving is taking on the responsibility of understanding other people.

Another thing that can get in the way is our inability to forgive. Therefore, we need to actively practice mercy and compassion. Mercy is necessary for us to use our discretionary power to overlook and forgive. It is in our power to instantly show leniency to a person's indiscretions and misstatements while they are attempting to communicate. We all have the ability to be selfish, especially if we are excited or in a hurry. One of my constant verbal flubs when I'm in a hurry is to say something like, "Pick up the thing and put it on the deal." When we are trying to explain something, we and others might use the wrong word. Mercy lets the wrong word be ignored, resulting in a more empathetic response.

Compassion, on the other hand, signals a strong desire to alleviate the uncertainty of another while they are trying to be understood. Selflessly giving mercy and compassion allows us to understand beyond normal human comprehension. We can ignore the distractions and focus on the real issue or problem. This works like seeing through the trees, smelling the wonderfulness of where we are, and being able to enjoy the beautiful snowcapped mountains beyond the trees.

Selflessly giving mercy and compassion is a rare type of kindheartedness which reflects a clear concern for others. It is a process making us attractive to others. People want to be around us because they are heard, they hear us, and we then come to know one another in a deep and understanding way. This shows giving of our time and attention lets others become affirmed.

When our opponents of Verbal Chess receive mercy and compassion this becomes a special and unique experience because it is rare. This gives them the ability to step back and analyze themselves. Our empathetic reflection slices through the misconceptions others may have of us. We radiate an undeniable light that makes our opponent sit up and notice. Later, our opponents may lie about what was said, but they will know in their hearts the undeniable truth about our motives.

When this connection is gained, people know we care as deeply for them as we do for ourselves. Projecting this truthful image during a stressful or meaningful conversation is an unbeatable combination. We create the opportunity for others to view us as truthful, compassionate people who will go to great lengths to understand. It is a phenomenon so rare it works like a magnet. People are drawn to us because they feel safe and rewarded, like a ship in a safe harbor when the storm rages outside.

When we gain this great ability to selflessly give mercy and compassion, we can receive a reverence from others beyond our wildest dreams. It is an experience arrogant people seek and can never sustain because it is all about them and their true motives are exposed. The reward of reverence from others can only be gained and sustained through selflessly giving grace.

Giving is the key to this phenomenon, because giving offers others the opportunity to give back. Giving our time and attention confirms it is not about us; it is all about them! When it is all about them, we are exercising the King's persona of integrity, humility, patience, forgiveness, self-control, and hope that gives us perseverance, combined with the spirit of the Queen's grace and empathy.

Great communicators project this image, and one of the greatest was President Reagan. He was even called the Great Communicator. He would stop and talk to the gardener and value this conversation as much as he would a conversation with the Ambassador of China. This is so unusual because politicians are always looking over the shoulder to find someone with more power and influence. Owning this duty transforms our focus from self-edification to valuing every word of another. It gives the person we are talking to value. Valuing what they think as much as we value what we think is giving them grace.

Great painters use the compassion part of grace to understand the person they are about to paint. The greatest painters have the ability to mentally step into their subject's life and paint the essence of their feelings. Art critics, when viewing an artist's painting, can see the subject's feelings in the painting. They also see into the painter's personality. Therefore, when the painter mentally steps into the subject to be painted, he paints his insight of the subject and in the process reveals a true part of himself as well.

Through the Queen's grace, like a critic viewing the artist's painting, we start to see ourselves more clearly, more truthfully, and gain greater insight of ourselves. This clearer vision of ourselves enables us to adjust our strategy to reflect the essence of the Queen's grace on our opponent during Verbal Chess. This is the pursuit of harmony and understanding, which is as great an achievement in communication as can be gained. Herein rests one of the truths of the Queen's grace and its complex nature.

Reality is the truth we are seeking. When we give the Queen's grace, we reveal our own true natures. We are able to better understand those who are most difficult to understand. This ability to accurately understand is crucial or our responses will be misdirected. This lack of accuracy explains why most people don't communicate well. It also explains one of the main reasons why some relationships break down and why some are strong. It is why marriage counselors list the inability to communicate as one of the primary reasons for the breakdown of marriages.

The Queen's grace, when it becomes part of our persona, also moves mountains of past psychological baggage. It makes those who have doubted us re-examine our motives and they start to question their negative conclusions. Then, if we say the wrong words, but the other person understands our honorable motives, they can forgive us and move on, giving us mercy.

The Queen's grace is a peacemaker that brings people together in an undeniable way that fosters trust, faith, and hope. It is the essence of love. Peacemaking is what happens when psychologists, priests, and pastors bring people together to better understand each other. Grace is the barrier jumper to true understanding, and we so desperately need this tool when everything else goes wrong. Yes, understanding and being understood occur because the Queen's grace is selflessly giving mercy and compassion.

Please note, a peacemaker is not a push over, or a peace wisher, a peace dreamer, or a peace talker. A peacemaker is an empathic truth-talker who gives compassion and mercy but finds a way to reveal the truth. Many people today are trying to be peacekeepers, not peacemakers. They believe peace at any cost will prevent arguments or conflict. This is wrongheaded, because the Queen of Verbal Chess is a bold peacemaker who stands in the gap and confronts evil with truth's compassion and mercy.

The Queen's grace can directly affect the hearts of other people, the centers of their human spirits from which spring emotions, thoughts, motivation, courage, and action. The Queen's grace is like time: we can't see time or touch it, but we certainly live by it. The Queen's empathic grace displayed through the King's character is time tested. It is the spirit of the communication game, a special faith revealed, enabling us to communicate with almost anyone. It lets our goodness show through and enables us to understand loved ones, clients, sales prospects, employees, spouse, our children, and friends. We can even understand those we don't care for and who seem unlovable.

When I was interviewing the Indian woman, I was giving her all four steps of the Queens grace, and I was doing it unselfishly. True, I didn't know what else to do, but in not knowing what to do, I fell unknowingly back on the Queen's grace which works almost every time. Think of it, if we could truly understand and influence the difficult, the unlovable, the arrogant, and provide a way for them to understand us, wouldn't our employment, family life, and all our relationships become better?

Lasting influence is generated by giving the Queen's grace. It is the engine that starts the winning process. It is the test of how well we can manage any situation. And it is only through the King's character, in conjunction with spirit of giving the Queen's grace, we find the truth and are able to act on it in a positive and edifying way. The truth says, "A generous man (a giving person) will prosper; he who refreshes others will himself be refreshed."[59]

When we start learning to use the Queen's grace it becomes habit-forming. You're going to want to know everybody's interior dynamics. When we see the positive effect giving grace has on others, it gives us a great feeling of satisfaction and joy. In action, it generates in us an innately powerful inner drive that feeds us with an insatiable desire to create close and caring relationships. The Queen's grace absorbs tension, enhances relationships, creates strong friendships, and permits us to have the chance to sail through life without the added difficulties we self-create. We literally take the self-centered drag off our personality when we give the Queen's grace.

The heart of the matter is our lives will truly get better, more rewarding, while giving the Queens grace. We can touch others in a meaningful way literally stripping away the barriers that stop a satisfying relationship.

The saddest people I talk to are focused on self. They have swallowed the lie, "It is all about me," hook, line, and sinker. Their lives are mostly filled with self-gratification and self-edification. The Book of Truth warns those who "lead a life of wanton pleasure [self-indulgence, self-gratification]; you have fattened your hearts in a day of slaughter."[60] These people's relationships are shallow like a baby pool. We really can't get into it, and when we do, we look ridiculous. They miss the joy of giving grace, the recognition of the King of integrity, the freedom of self-control, the peace of forgiveness, the admiration of humility, the gift of gratitude, the affection of acceptance, the affirming nature of patience, the reward of faith, and the resolve of hope that gives us perseverance. The Queen's grace is the truthful projection of a righteous person who is caring, virtuous, and compassionate, but doesn't think they are caring, virtuous, or compassionate enough. They are the master communicators of the world because they are not only heard, they truly understand, and are truly understood.

The bestselling book of all time describes how the earth was formed and how people are to live. The Book reveals the persona of evil as the focus on self and the persona of righteousness as the magnification of unselfishness. Nothing said was ever truer! If we cannot strive to have the character of the King and give the grace of the Queen, we don't stand a chance of getting others to listen to us, much less accept our ideas.

When dispensing the Queen's empathy, we are like water to a thirsty person. Like a mirror we reflect a caring compassionate human face, so the brightness of the King's character shines through. This view is the image of the King with the spirit of Queen. It causes the wellspring of life to open in other people. It is truly the key to the door leading to the master communicator within us. This is probably the most important concept of communication.

Without giving the Queen's grace we can have influence, but we will not inspire. We may focus on achievement but garner no lasting success. We will try but we will not be trusted, succeed but not triumph, use power but we will not win the hearts and minds of others.

The Queen: The Skill of Giving Grace

The Anti-Queen

The Queen's grace is not sympathy, anger, fear, or apathy; these all come from the Anti-Queen, which is the dark side of communication and our opponent. The Anti-Queen "lets us become self-absorbed, conceited, provoking one another, and envying one another."[61]

Sympathy is a condition in which one induces a parallel or reciprocal condition in another. In other words, we get into the other person's fishbowl and start relating our problems with their problems. We go to self when we give sympathy and say self-regarding things like, "I know exactly how you feel." However through empathy we can relate and try to understand others, but we cannot know exactly how others feel.

A good example of this is a fire chaplain I met in one of my trainings. He told me when he was new to his position he would meet with people who had lost a loved one and would instinctively go to sympathy relating how he felt about death when his mother died. A widow he was trying to comfort looked at him and said, "That's sad how you feel, but today I'm dealing with my husband's death." This statement hit him like a baseball bat between the eyes. He told me the widow was telling the truth. He wasn't dealing with her grief because he was seeing himself and relating to his past grief. He had to attempt to step back out of himself to see and feel her feelings. Then he could interpret her feelings of pain in an unbiased way. We have to be able to mentally step back and see reality or we get pulled into sympathy, or worse, we can go the opposite direction to irritation or anger. Always remember, the Queen's grace is not about us, it is all about others.

Anger is similar to sympathy in the way it is all about us and keeps us from seeing reality. Remember the story about the attorney who lost it? His actions were all about him, and not about solving the problem at hand. The investigation I completed must have made him look bad so he acted on his anger instead of trying to understand where he could have gone wrong. The result of his outburst was devastating to his reflection. If we let our emotions get control, we are seen as weak which can be humiliating.

In an intense encounter, it is critically important to slow down in order to avoid being caught up in emotions. Luckily, I slowed things down in that conference room showdown and was able to show the King's persona and the Queen's grace. When we consciously try to slow things down, we let grace express itself and arm ourselves with the King's self-control. Slowing things down helps regain composure and keeps us from taking the bait of anger and letting go of our self-control.

Fear and apathy are additional Anti-Queen attributes which can move us away from understanding. Fear (we're talking about fear in conversations) is truly all about us and, like anger, if we slow things down mentally, we can go back to the truth of reality. We understand that fear of rejection, fear of verbal assault, or fear of the unknown is usually based on the history of communication with the opponent. Giving the Queen's grace can move us past fear to an enlightenment that quells uncertainties.

Reality, arrived at through self-control, makes us understand we can influence the end-result. Self-control lets us focus on the real goal of our conversation or actions and not on uncertainties. Our focus on the real goal helps motivate us to maintain self-control. However, we must be aware that a history of past uncomfortable experiences, or imagined adverse results, reinforces false evidence that appears real: *fear.*

The Queen: The Skill of Giving Grace

Apathy is also an Anti-Queen attribute and the opposite of empathic grace. Apathy just doesn't care. Apathy is one of the biggest reasons people don't communicate, because an uncaring attitude kills the desire to communicate. Some people believe apathy cannot be changed, but when I hear this I ask: do others have control over your happiness? Can we choose to have a good day versus a bad day, or be in a bad mood or not? Can we be kind when we don't feel kindness? Yes, we can will ourselves to care, will ourselves to be happy, and will ourselves to be in a good mood. If we are in control, we use our minds, hearts, and willpower to control our mouths and actions. We become inflow enablers and strategic outflow experts.

In revealing the total persona of the Anti-Queen we must understand this is the evil side of communication and it can come from us or from our opponent. People who use the evil side can be dangerous or lead us to the dark side where the evil empire strikes back as in the movie *Star Wars*. These people use what I call functional or fake grace versus authentic grace. The Queen's grace is looking out for the opponent of Verbal Chess. Functional grace is used by people who are putting on an act to trick or con people into doing something the con wants them to do. Therefore, functional grace is the motive behind the end justifies the means. The end we seek can then self-justify any unrighteous act.

To stay away from being conned or tricked by functional grace we must know our longings. Our longings reveal the empty spaces in our lives that can make us vulnerable. A simple example: if we long for a new car and cannot afford one, we shouldn't go into a new car dealership. A sharp salesman will identify those longings and give us as much functional grace as we need to purchase the new vehicle. Some salespeople, like con-men, will try to be your best friend. So, beware of uninvited intimacy. When strangers or others who do not know us ask intimate personal questions, beware. Intimacy doesn't occur suddenly and anyone who tries to make it happen after a few moments of conversation has something other than your best interest in mind.

There are people we should keep at arm's length. Especially be aware of blamers. Blamers are the antonym of the Queen of Verbal Chess. Blaming is taking compassion and mercy and throwing it in the trash can.

What is happening inside a blamer's mind? When their behavior does not produce the desired results, it creates a one-way inflow reaction of self-protection. Their delusional self cannot be taken down. This is where the downward blame process kicks in; instead of taking responsibility they conclude they should be excused from the repercussions, because they believe they are above them. The blaming mindset is a slippery slope we can all fall into. Blaming is so close to complaining it is difficult to self-recognize because it is self-reinforcing. They even become the person they are complaining about. In short, many do not know they are blaming because it seems logical and normal to them. Like all high-risk self-serving behaviors, blaming brings short term gratification. But the resulting long-term mistrust blaming generates can be fatal to productive conversations.

Complaining is systematic in some organizations. This happens not because people are always unhappy. It just seems they don't have anything else to talk about.

Years ago, when I was an FBI agent in Chicago, several of us would go out to breakfast a couple of days a week and complain about our jobs. One of the agents had served two tours in Viet Nam as a Marine officer. One day he told us a story of how a group of Viet Cong snuck a 50-caliber machinegun within one hundred yards of his position and opened fire. My friend was forced to dive into a ditch filled with sewage that you wouldn't want to even put a finger in because it smelled so bad. He tried to get his entire body into the ditch as the bullets exploded around him. After my friend finished his story, he looked around the table and said, "Guys, if it's not that bad, it's not that bad." That ended our complaining.

How many times have we heard someone use the Anti-Queen and try to redirect blame by complaining about someone or something else? Have we done this? Maybe we've said something mean and hurtful, or committed a verbally destructive act and justified our behavior by saying the person was the cause, or they made us mad, or . . . ? This is like saying the devil made me do it.

Unfortunately, blame is like anger; it takes away one's compassion and mercy for others. It allows a person to act in a hurtful way to another human being without the consequence of feeling we did something wrong. Humans, by nature have inhibitions, which are learned responses that serve as a buffer against what they know is bad or self-serving behavior. Blame—and complaining, for that matter—are self-learned behaviors which are difficult to control, allowing the person's emotions to override their self-control to achieve a rationalized selfish end. This can include possibly violent behavior.

The Anti-Queen also uses self-serving re-interpretations. They use emotions that are merciless to inflame people to further their own self-serving ends or needs. They create doubts and bogus feelings to start forest fires. These Anti-Queen remarks lack compassion by overemphasizing themselves while at the same time under-emphasizing others. Some have narcissistic personality disorders. Many are just egotistical, their lives based on self-gratification through deflecting the consequences of their actions. They simply accuse others or create implausible situations to exclude themselves from repercussions by selfishly deflecting blame. The Book of Truth says, "[A]cts of the flesh are obvious: they manifest selfish ambition, through dissension, discord, hatred, heresies, fornication, murders, drunkenness, and factions."[62]

Conclusion

The Queen is the skill of giving grace, thereby achieving understanding by being sensitive to and vicariously experiencing the feelings, thoughts, and knowledge of others. The Queen fully communicates this in an empathetic and clear way. The Queen is able to step back and view the whole picture with the intent of acting graciously on new understandings by being positive and edifying.

By projecting the Queen's grace, we place ourselves in a position to gain as complete an understanding as humanly possible by empathetically interpreting the inner-most feelings of another. Then we can feel the pleasure of being empathetic because we have gained the controlled insight, showing a positive countenance, saying positive words in edifying ways. These positive words display understanding and affirm the other person. Therefore, "Command and teach these things. . . . set an example for the others in speech, in conduct, in life, in faith and in purity."[63]

We must not forget that without giving the Queen's grace, we can have influence, but we will not inspire; have achievement, but not lasting success. We will try but we will not be trusted; succeed but not triumph; use power but we will not win the hearts and minds of others.

6
The Bishop

EMPATHETIC LISTENING

SO FAR, WE have discussed the traits of the King and the Queen, who are the royalty in the game of Verbal Chess. Remember, the King represents our virtues, while the Queen represents our motives (grace). If we want to be successful in communicating with others, we must have both the King's virtues and the Queen's grace. In utilizing these traits, we have the opportunity to re-create ourselves. We have all said and done things in the past that we regret. Our reputations may have suffered as a result. But as we develop the King's virtues and the Queen's grace, we gain trust with others and start to rebuild our reputations with them. Virtue and grace are the good fruit produced by the Royals of Verbal Chess. Therefore, we need to gain the persona of the Royals to be Master Communicators.

This leads us to the next piece on the board: The Bishop. The Bishop represents the way we gather information in the "game." The Bishop is moving diagonally across the playing field, searching out, anticipating, and seeking to understand our opponent's most important inner feelings.

The most difficult part of Verbal Chess and the third most important discipline is learning to listen. I truly admire those who listen naturally, because to most of us, listening is unnatural. Listening is the first key to all meaningful communication. Therefore, Verbal Chess players must be listening champions to win the game of life, the art of speaking life into others.

The Book of Truth written over two thousand years ago encourages us to, "Listen before you answer. If you don't, you are being unwise and insulting."[64] This is again confirmed, "He who answers before listening [to the facts], that is his folly and shame."[65] These undeniable truths enable us to overcome foolhardiness and help us learn the concepts of the Bishop of Verbal Chess.

What makes empathetic listening difficult is that for every two people having a conversation there are three different identities on each side. The first identity is our real self, the second is how we see ourselves, and third is how we are seen by the other person.

The question is, can we see ourselves exactly how other people see us? Does Mr. Know Everything, or Mrs. Obstinate truly know how they are seen? How about Mr. Pliable or Mrs. Gossip—do they know? Then consider one of the worst, Mr. Never Stops Talking—does he see himself truly? The answer is almost certainly no. If perception is truth, in every two-person conversation there are two perceived people and one real person on each side.

This is why replicating the role of the Bishop's empathetic listening, is so important. An empathetic individual in Verbal Chess is defined as a person who is commiserative, compassionate, humane, kind, and blessed with an overabundance of self-control. The antonym is a person who fails at listening because they are angry, arrogant, hard-hearted, self-absorbed, heartless, unfeeling, or pathetic. Then "Everyone should be quick to listen, slow to speak, and slower to become angry."[66]

The nature of the royalty of Verbal Chess embraces self-control and giving grace as explained in the preceding chapters. Self-control is when maturity precedes longings, instant gratification, imagined needs, and uncontrolled speaking, etc. It is also the key to our ability to listen through compassion which requires giving unmerited mercy in order to be successful. Listening, which is refraining from speaking, enables us to have the strength and strategy to succeed. We must understand we either follow the strategy of the Bishop, or happenstance. Happenstance is the part of our persona that entices our lower nature leading us to folly and shame. The Book of Truth says, "Let the wise listen and add to their learning, and let the discerning get guidance."[67] Therefore, to succeed as the Bishop of Verbal Chess we must learn to desecrate our uncontrolled tendencies.

Four Kinds of Communication

There are four traditional kinds of communication: reading, writing, speaking, and listening. How many years do we spend learning to read, write, and speak? We go to school, many to college, and some take other classes, read books, etc., on how to read, write, and speak. When do we learn how to listen?

Very seldom in our lives do we take a class on how to listen empathetically. This is why, in Verbal Chess, the Bishop is the most valuable intelligence gatherer on the playing field. We desperately need to learn how to use the Bishop because empathetic listening is an unnatural, highly artistic discipline used to read our opponents, anticipate their actions, and understand their points of view. The Bishop empowers us to create an instant strategy to win the game of life, the art of speaking life into others.

To learn how to empathetically listen we must know how we typically listen. Normally, humans listen to be understood. Therefore, to be understood, when the other person is speaking we are ordinarily rehearsing what we are going to say when it is our turn to talk. This is acting like we are listening, while we half-listen. We may be sitting or standing, looking at our opponent, but all the while thinking about what we are going to say. When we are talking, our opponent is thinking about what they are going to say. Nobody on either side is truly listening and we are all amazed when we do not understand each other.

The opposite of listening is not talking, but waiting to interrupt. This is how most of us listen. Worse, many times we give our life story, or relate a particular incident or truth. We may have told this story hundreds of times and do not remember if we are repeating ourselves because we are on autopilot, which is talking without listening. This falls within the valley of the Anti-Bishop.

I love telling the following story because it is probably the instant in my personal life when I found out my views were not as important as I thought. It is also the point that I realized I was acting like Mr. Long Talker and nobody was listening because I was emulating the Anti-Bishop of Verbal Chess.

I was walking past my daughter's bedroom when I heard my name. I stopped and put my ear to the door and heard my older daughter telling my younger daughter, "Now, when Dad gives you his lectures, I want you to look at him, like I do, and count his gray hairs. He will never guess you are not listening." Wow, was that embarrassing. I was saying what I wanted my daughters to hear, giving them my own rehearsed wisdom, and never understanding what was going on inside my daughters' minds.

Therefore, if we do not empathetically listen to people and watch their total countenance, we don't really have a clue if they are listening or understanding us. Through this experience, and many others I am embarrassed to talk about, I learned that empathetic listening is a very rewarding strategic move of the Bishop of Verbal Chess.

When Others Speak, We Listen at Five Levels

So, what are the signs that we are not actually listening to the other person? I believe there are five ways that we only "half-listen."

First—Ignoring

We just don't care, and we are not listening. This is the Anti-Bishop.

Second—Pretend listening

We say things like, "Yeah. Right! Yep. Uh-huh." I give this example, because when I was watching the Super Bowl years ago, my daughter's five-year-old little girl, came up to me saying, "Grandpa, can I tell you a story?" "Yeah, sure, yeah!" She's telling the story and I'm going, "Yeah! Yeah! Oh wow! Touchdown!" As I jump out of my chair with my hands in the air. "Oh, excuse me darling, what did you say?" I was pretending to listen and by the look on her face, it hurt. This is the truth of the Anti-Bishop.

Third—Selective listening

This is where the conversation is either about a topic we are not interested in or, we have heard the story before. We have already made up our minds, and don't believe or care to hear it again. The selective listener cuts and pastes selective parts of what they want to hear, from what they do not want to hear. After we have heard all we want to hear, we revert to pretend listening.

Fourth—Attentive listening

Attentive listening is paying attention, but focusing just on words. This is like talking to someone on the phone. We can only focus on words. Humans have some of the biggest misunderstandings when listening to just words.

Years ago, when I was moving my family from Sacramento to Santa Rosa, California, I was looking for a home. My wife was in Sacramento and the only way I could tell her about the homes I was considering was on the phone. I tried to describe the good and the bad, but we ended up arguing. I realized I was trying to paint a verbal picture of the homes, and she had no way to see it with just words. Words are only ten percent of communication; tone of voice is thirty percent. But words and tone do not see feelings during meaningful conversations because sixty percent of communication is seeing with our eyes.

The Book of Truth explains the power of listening with our eyes,

> . . . they hardly hear with their ears, and they have closed their eyes. Otherwise they might see with their eyes, hear with their ears, and understand with their hearts . . . But blessed are your eyes because they see, and your ears because they hear.[68]

This indicates all meaningful communication should be done in person if we truly want to vicariously experience the feelings and thoughts of another.

Fifth—Empathetic listening is the Bishop of Verbal Chess

What is empathetic listening? Simply, it is listening with empathy. We reviewed giving grace, the Queen of Verbal Chess. The Queen is getting inside the other person's life, giving them compassion and mercy so we might see things through their eyes. The only way we really get inside is through empathetic listening. Empathetic listening is the act of understanding by vicariously experiencing the feelings, and thoughts of another through sight and sound. In other words, unless we actually try to grasp others' feelings, and understand them, there's no way we can really know what they are meaning. Empathetic listening requires focusing in and paying attention, not only to the words being spoken, but also to the gestures, general posture, body position, and facial expressions.

While visiting my nephew and his wife, I discovered they were having marital problems. We went out to dinner and after my nephew got up and left for the bathroom, I asked her how they were doing. She said, "We're doing just fine." But using the Bishop's empathetic listening with my eyes and ears her reply went like this: when I asked, she put her fork down, at the same moment her eyes looked down, and her shoulders slightly sagged, as she said, with a normal tone then a short pause, ending with decreasing volume when saying fine. "We're doing just fine?" The *fine* should have been a crescendo when she said, "We're doing just *fine.*" Now let's ask ourselves, are they doing just fine? No! Seeing her body language and hearing her tone of voice enabled me to see the truth was the opposite of what she said. This was only possible through empathic listening.

When we listen with empathy, we make a conscious effort to set aside our biases. Biases can be the largest obstacles to listening. What are biases? When we say to ourselves, "I've heard this person before, and nothing he or she says makes sense." That is bias, and it comes in many forms. A bias is a personal and sometimes unreasoned judgment in which we draw a conclusion or make an assumption about a person or event that may or may not be true.

Pre-conclusions leading to assumptions make us into the Anti-Bishop. Remember how A-S-S-U-M-E is spelled? When we assume, it will make a-you-know-what out of you and me. When I was going through FBI training school, an instructor of investigations wrote the word *assume* on the chalkboard. He said, "Boys," in his Irish accent, "If you start assuming, you are no longer an investigator, you have become a politician." I laugh at this today, but it's true. When we are listening empathetically, we are investigators and we assume nothing while we are intently listening. Hence, we can arrive at as much truth as possible versus an assumption.

Active Listening

Total communication, as I related, is composed of ten percent words, thirty percent sounds, and sixty percent body language. This is so important to understand. If we don't realize this, we start drifting away when people are talking. How many times have we walked into a situation where we start talking to somebody and they go, "Uh-huh, uh-huh," and turn away from us? They are pretend listening. We must listen with our eyes and ears to see feelings to be successful at listening and we need to do it every time. We cannot have something that may distract us like a remote control. Men, when talking to your wives, make sure you do not have a remote in your hand. This is a bad mistake because the remote non-verbally displays what is important. Also, please do not think we can mute the TV and have a meaningful conversation. If we just glance at the TV during our conversation we may humiliate our wives or others. Personally, when I engage in a meaningful conversation, or my wife wants to talk, I imagine myself putting on my listening hat. After I imagine this, I am ready to listen.

I will tell a little secret: empathetic listening is risky in a sense. When we start to listen empathetically, we start giving of ourselves by giving grace, the Queen. When this happens, all of a sudden we are seen by others in a new, positive light. Additionally, our emotions can play tricks on us. We will start getting inside of others' feelings and our own too. Getting inside the minds of others is honestly starting to understand the person we are listening to. In one sense, this is hard because normally we don't want to go that deep. I'll warn you, once we start to empathetically listen, it becomes addictive. We start developing the persona of royalty and more people will want to be around us, like my daughter who started telling her mother, "Dad is so understanding." Was Dad really understanding? No! I didn't understand everything my daughter said, but I did understand myself better. I did this by empathetically listening as I affirmed my daughter, and our relationship grew. One receives this profit by emulating the Bishop of Verbal Chess.

When we know through our own experience the power of this kind of listening, we begin to grasp how the ability to listen brings us closer, strengthens our relationships, and lets us understand ourselves. Understanding ourselves? Yes, when we honestly start giving our total attention, we start truthfully understanding ourselves. And this is one of the best outcomes of all, for as we comprehend how great a gift this is, we see the importance of extending it to others. We start relishing the ability to affirm them.

Empathetic listening is so powerful because it gives us the most accurate intelligence we can obtain. Just think about this for a minute or two. While we are having a meaningful conversation, we are receiving as much accurate information as possible instead of projecting your own autobiography or sales pitch, making assumptions, or focusing on reinterpretations. This is the insight we need to gain in order to become Master Communicators. When the opponent feels affirmed while we are listening, we are disarming our opponent and winning with the Bishop of Verbal Chess.

Sympathy versus Empathetic Listening

As a word of caution, empathetic listening is not synonymous with sympathy. Sympathy is the inclination or having the capacity to share the feelings of another. Empathy goes to understanding what others are experiencing by having the capacity to experience the feelings of another. Sympathy, like empathy, enables us to see and feel what the other person is feeling but this is where we hit the fork in the road. Sympathy is about a quarter of an inch from empathy sitting side by side until they split. Sympathy is connecting everything the other person relates to our own experiences and then relating them back through our thoughts and feelings. Something like, "I understand exactly how you feel." This is where we make a big mistake, because we cannot fully understand how another person feels.

When we fall into the pit of sympathy, this is where we change our focus to ourselves and stop listening. Sympathy is a barrier to empathetic listening. If you want to hear sympathy, go to a few funerals. Listen with your eyes as people try to express comfort through sympathy. To the wife who has lost her husband, people will sometimes say the most ridiculous things (even unknowingly hurtful things) trying to comfort the grieving.

The wife is standing at the gathering after the funeral, and she is weeping softly. Her children are all weeping, and their body language displays a depressed state of grief. A person walks up trying to comfort and show sympathy, and says, "He's probably in a better place." Wow, they have just lost their loved one. They don't want to hear this. Maybe a different lady walks up and says to the wife, "I lost my husband, and I know exactly how you feel." Is this comforting? Let's try another insulting one, "You will slowly get over it, so don't worry." That hurts. Then the best uncaring one yet, "You'll probably be better off without him."

There was no comfort for the grieving in those statements. They showed no true empathy. They failed because without empathetic listening they went to sympathy, which is being more concerned with how they themselves feel than showing empathy for the grieved.

Physical versus Psychological Survival

Next to physical survival the greatest human need is psychological survival. In my lifetime, I have done a lot of scuba diving and I can confirm the greatest physical need is air. Then after we secure air, maybe second and third are water and food become our greatest *physical needs*.

I cannot emphasize enough that people who learn how to listen have great power. The greatest psychological need is to be heard and understood, which is to be affirmed. This is so powerful! It is beyond our imagination. When we can sit down and fully listen to somebody, especially someone we love, and give them their greatest psychological need, it turns into a wonderful gift beyond our imagination. We are providing this gift by giving our time, our patience, and our concern all wrapped around affirmation. We are stepping into their lives with our undivided attention and trying to see what they see through their eyes. Then, at the same time, we can step back and see the reality of the situation from the outside. We haven't gone to sympathy, we haven't given them our story; all we have done is deeply listen to them.

This is a kind of "holy listening."

> We can give only what we have received. We receive by listening and assimilating. The word to which we respond is the word which is heard, not just with our ears, but more deeply through our eyes: inside us, where love and will abide, where we decide what we will do.[69]

Empathetic listening is listening another soul into life, into a condition of disclosure and discovery. This is maybe the greatest psychological service any human can ever perform for another. Just think about how wonderful a gift we are giving when we honestly listen people into a condition of disclosure.

A great example: my daughter used to come into my room after she got back from work, sit at the end of the bed, and tell me about her day. I made the mistake of selectively listening, then trying to verbally fix her problems. She would leave frustrated with me. When I finally started truly listening, I got two revelations. One, I was being tasked with affirming my daughter by listening, not fixing. I started really seeing my daughter in the light and telling my wife, "You know, she is really smart!" I just had to empathetically listen to get there, and then the best thing happened, the second revelation. She told her mother how her dad was starting to become so very understanding.

The Deepest Psychological Hurt is Humiliation

If we want to humiliate someone, just play like we are listening when they are serious. This is one of the worst forms of humiliation. It is the opposite of empathetic listening because we are saying without speaking that they are not valued, or important enough to be listened to.

Conclusion

Poor listening, the Anti-Bishop, reveals that the listener either does not know the value of listening, has a low regard for what others have to say, or is too self-absorbed with internal noise to listen. Striving to exemplify the Bishop of Verbal Chess is being self-taught—

> . . . with regard to your former way of life, put off your old self, which is being corrupted by its selfish desires; to be made new in the attitude of your minds; and to put on the new self . . .[70]

The effect of not listening to others is humiliating them and painting yourself in a bad light. When we deny affirmation to others, we are not going to be well-liked. We should never forget people who do not listen; they not only will die without knowledge, but they die without ever affirming others. The Good Book confirms this, "The way of fools seems right to them, but the wise listen."[71]

7

The Knight

STRATEGIC SPEAKING

THE BOOK OF Truth tells us, "Let no unwholesome word proceed from your mouth, but only such a word as is good for the edification according to the need of the moment, that it may give grace to those who hear."[72] To put this in everyday language we should not allow low empathy words to proceed from our mouths, but only such words good for edification. Our words should give grace, the Queen of Verbal Chess, according to the need of the moment, and selflessly give mercy and compassion through the persona of the King of Verbal Chess. "One . . . who speaks with grace will have many a friend."[73]

Strategic speaking—the Knight—is our verbal personality and the most unique motion piece in the game of Verbal Chess. It jumps over or moves around our opponent to beneficially influence them. The Knight, used correctly, is key to successful communication. If used incorrectly it becomes the Anti-Knight, the avenue for failure in Verbal Chess.

The Knight of Verbal Chess is the strategic speaking piece of the game of communication. It displays our emotional intelligence. Emotional intelligence sometimes means being silent, as the Book of Truth says, "Even fools are thought wise if they keep silent, and discerning if they hold their tongues."[74]

The Knight: Strategic Speaking

Strategic speaking is a learned skill shaped by life experiences. It is controlled by the knowledge that the greater responsibility for understanding is on the speaker. This is learning the ability to speak to understand. This is speaking to put ourselves in other people's shoes while using compassionate empathy. This enables us to understand as much as possible a person's thoughts and feelings. Empathetic people try to imagine themselves in another's place in order to understand what others are feeling or experiencing. Empathy facilitates verbal intelligence which comes from within so we behave in a more compassionate way. Emotional intelligence projects empathy.

Those lacking emotional intelligence (empathy) are people who have a short supply of concern for others. This is what I call the Empathy Deficiency Syndrome or EDS. People who suffer from this deficiency have few lasting relationships because, lacking empathy, they knowingly or unknowingly promote frustration, anger, disappointment, and betrayal, leaving others feeling at the very least, unsettled.

There are three types of verbal empathy, High, Low, and Medium

High Empathy is Verbal Enhancement

High empathy is used to expound, make an important point, or to tell a story while play talking. Play talking is when we are having fun conversing with friends or acquaintances with like hobbies or interests. High empathy verbalizes feelings and experiences with descriptive remarks, verbal enhancements, and many times talks over our fellow communicators. This is play talking and at this point, it is not strategic speaking.

An instance where high empathy becomes very productive is when warning someone of danger. It is when we see a car running a red light and we are trying to tell the driver the danger.

On the other hand, high empathy becomes very unproductive when we use it to discourage the other person from sharing. This is dominating the conversation. A simple example is if someone says, "It's raining outside." Then the person expressing high empathy would say: "It's really raining hard. When I left home it was pouring and I got all wet when my umbrella broke, and I could hardly get into work without getting soaked," and then they go on and on.

However, high empathy when dominating a conversation lacks understanding and destroys the goals of Verbal Chess. If, in a meaningful conversation, like a sales meeting, a person dominates the conversation, he/she is losing at Verbal Chess. Sales can be simply finding a need and recommending solutions through provided services or products. Dominating the conversation with verbal overflow does not discover the need for services or products, and loses the game of Verbal Chess.

The following is a good example of when high empathy can be negative because it leads a person to share too much "friendly" type of talk, rather than listen. I took a new employee to a sales call—my bad. I took it for granted that he would know to watch and stay silent. It took several weeks to arrange this meeting with the CEO of a company that I thought may need our services. The CEO was a big-time game hunter. He had a lot of stuffed African big game heads in his office. My employee was also a hunter. The communication started with the CEO talking about his hunting experiences. Then my employee took off with his own hunting stories, taking up too much of our limited time. I was watching the CEO's silent communication and could see he was not impressed.

I couldn't get a word in edgewise and the CEO started looking at his watch. My employee was clueless to this because he was having so much fun telling everyone what a great hunter he was. The CEO then excused himself saying he needed to take a call. We left his office, and I asked my employee to step outside. When we got outside, I handed him the car keys and told him to go and sit in the vehicle until I was through. I went back and tried to talk to the CEO but he was engaged in another phone call, and I lost the opportunity for the sales meeting.

This kind of verbal enhancement discourages the Verbal Chess opponent/client from speaking. It's Mr. Long Talker who is doing all the talking, whose uncaring lack of empathy has no problem keeping others from speaking. After all, in their mind it's all about them.

Imagine we make an appointment with our boss to discuss a work problem, and after we get the first few words out of our mouth he or she takes off and never stops talking for the rest of the meeting. Their high empathy engaged and they started telling us not only what they think, but many times what we think. They explain how high they jumped to solve similar problems though we are never fully able to describe the real problem. This is expressing high empathy during strategic conversations. It not only destroys productive communication, but it also destroys identifying possible solutions. This is where teamwork is ruined, and our work product suffers.

This type of pathetic empathy can also be present in our homes and in our relationships with our spouse and children. I did a little counseling with a married couple. When we got together the wife started using high empathy. For a full five minutes she told me not only what their problem was, but what her husband's problem was. She named the times, places, and events where her husband had failed in their relationship. When I asked her what she did wrong, she immediately turned on her husband again. It was like the thought that she could be part of the problem was blocked from her mind. This is pathetic empathy, where a person is so self-concerned and self-justified that she or he cannot see the forest for the trees. This may be a blamer or an accuser who is not capable of looking at themselves in the mirror or seeing their own shortcomings.

The blamer simply accuses others of implausible situations to exclude themselves from repercussions by selfishly deflecting the blame. "The acts of the flesh are obvious: they manifest selfish ambition, through dissension, discord, hatred, heresies, fornication, murders, drunkenness, and factions."[75] Blaming is like anger, it takes away one's compassion and empathy for others. It allows a person to act in a harmful way to another without internal consequences. These people cannot win at the game of life, Verbal Chess.

Low Empathy—Killing the Conversation at Another's Expense

There are different types and ways of expressing low empathy. Low empathy can be uncaring, rude comments that cut our opponent to their knees and/or provoke confrontation. However, most humans suffer from selective low empathy, meaning they are not constantly rude or uncaring, just on certain occasions. This comes from the fact that all humans are inconsistent, complex, and flawed. This type of person chooses when to besmirch or slander their victims. This behavior is two-faced, for at times we act very empathetic, then, as our mood changes, we devalue others with words of scorn and ridicule. We have all heard the joke, "She or he can go from angel to evil in five seconds." Sadly, most humans can be self-serving actors with selective filters on their lips. Nevertheless, low empathy speech when engaged, can destroy relationships.

Another kind of low empathy is what I call the "Catch and Throw Back" statements. We all own a mitt to catch any dig, barb, or condescending remark. Then many of us will throw a low empathy fastball right back. We do this with more energy and darkness than was originally thrown to us. This is a revenge throwback statement. The key is to overcome the "Catch and Throw Back" and put an end to grabbing the mitt in the first place. This is a must if we want to play and win at Verbal Chess.

There was a time not long ago when it was raining cats and dogs, and I went through a stop sign. I saw it at the last moment and tried to stop but couldn't without sliding through the intersection. In an instant I looked both ways and, thankfully, nobody was coming. There was one car about a block away and it happened to be a sheriff's officer. He turned on his red light and I pulled over, thinking, shucks, I just got myself a ticket. These are moments when we are singing that old familiar song: dumb, dumb, I really did a dumb thing.

The sheriff's officer got out of his vehicle, and I was already standing next to my car in the rain. He said, "What do you think you are doing?" I replied that with the rain and everything, I wasn't paying good enough attention, and had really done a stupid thing. He immediately said, "You're right, you are stupid!"

He did not know I was a former FBI agent and had taught police officers communication. From then on, I only listened with my eyes (the Bishop of Verbal Chess) and answered questions yes or no. He not only killed the conversation, he made himself look like an egotistical imbecile.

When people use condescending low empathy, we conclude they are egotistical jerks who lack empathy for others. He needed to ask himself what profit was gained by verbally abusing me. He didn't need to agree or say anything; he could have just nodded his head to say he understood. If he would have been seeing with his eyes and hearing with his ears, he could have seen by my body language and tone of voice what took place was truly an accident.

Luckily for me he did not end up giving me a ticket. He went back to his car, checked out my license and finished by giving me another low empathy lecture. He looked like he was on autopilot verbalizing his rehearsed and often repeated condemnation. He was an egotistical individual who needed verbal acknowledgement to reinforce his self-importance. So, I found every way to be respectful and honor his ego and even thanked him several times before he left. (After this kind of conversation, we start spitting to get the taste of what we said out of our mouth.) It is repulsive sometimes when we have to deal with arrogant people, but to be successful communicators we need to project empathy, or we fail.

Low empathy is sometimes subtle, implied, or displayed through our body language. It is evident when looking at our total countenance. Low empathy is also displayed through our tone of voice, our pitch, and modulation. The sheriff's officer stood while addressing me with his legs apart (this is an aggressive stance), his hands on his hips, and the tone and cadence of his voice displayed superiority. His body language and speech revealed he was truly saying, "If you don't think I'm special and have power, then I'm here to prove it!" This is the definition of low empathy. We could all think of a few different words to call him. He thought he was superior, he talked like he was superior, and because of his position he abused his power through low empathy. There was no doubt that either I was going to bow, or he was going to give me a ticket. I did neither; I played him by respecting and pumping up his ego. Everything I said and did, was honoring his position, and helping him believe he was superior. It worked: I escaped getting a ticket. Truthfully, he was the only one who thought he was superior. The Book of Truth says, "The tongue is a fire, a world of evil among the parts of the body. It corrupts the whole body, sets the whole course of one's life on fire . . ."[76]

If we are having a conversation with somebody, and it's turning into a bit of a debate, and we are feeling very good about what we are saying because we are making the better of the conversation, chances are we are losing the game of Verbal Chess. Does this surprise you? Unless we are in an organized debate, if we are feeling we have one-upped the other person, we are probably losing. Once we start to feel we are winning it's a good possibility we are in a mild game of verbal warfare. We may even be using "Catch and Throw Back" statements.

When this happens, flags should start going up saying, *caution, caution!* This is where we tell ourselves, "I might be going the wrong way here, because I'm more concerned with winning than gaining respect!" It is time to start thinking about our strategy and asking ourselves what profit am I trying to gain? The minimum win of Verbal Chess is when we finish the conversation, our opponent has every opportunity to respect us. If we are not sure, it is time to start displaying the royalty of Verbal Chess.

Another way people speak in low empathy terms is by agreeing with negative comments towards somebody when others are conversing. I call this "echo criticizing" because we can hear it echoing off the canyon walls. We see this especially in teenagers, when the sister is being told by her mother that she did something wrong, and brother piles on by verbally agreeing. He is using low empathy with words like, "Yeah, she does it all the time." "It is about time," etc. This is echo criticizing, or uncontrolled ventilating to get back, or background revenge speaking. It is the mob mentality being displayed by our body language (nodding our head, using hand gestures), or by verbalizing, or anything people can come up with that throws gasoline on another's conversation to make it burn more brightly.

In the game of Verbal Chess there are several never-speaks that are low empathy phrases. Here are some examples of words or statements we should try to extract from our vocabulary.

- Ordering or instructing words (unless we are yelling a caution or disciplining children)—"Come here!" "Be reasonable." "Calm down!" These insult people's intelligence.

- Immovable excuses—"Because those are the rules!"

- Words which exclude—"It's none of your business."

- Humiliating words—"What's your problem?" "You wouldn't understand."

- Ultimatums—"Do this, or else!"

Low empathy statements such as these never enhance communication or lead to understanding. Instead, they enhance conflict.

Other never-speaks sometimes occur when asking about a person's involvement. Statements like, "You did this, or why didn't you do that, or why are you here?" are condescending, low empathy statements. We need to change the emphasis to a broader approach like, "I feel like this part wasn't completely done," or "How did the job go today?" These are more open-ended questions without low empathy. Another never-speak is if we restrict our explanations: "I'm not going to say this again," or "I've already told you."

Another example of low empathy is when someone replies, "Someone of my stature does not deal with these problems." They are similar to the sheriff's officer acting pious and arrogant with a heavy dose of verbal low empathy. All of these statements show a quality of pretend superiority. Masters of Communication should stay away from all these kinds of displays.

If we want to aggravate someone and start verbal warfare, all of the above statements work really well. However, we will not win in the game of life, Verbal Chess. In my life as a state senator, I never, never, use low empathy when I'm having a conversation. In the realm of instant news today, using low empathy statements is a bad idea. Also, with everyone having a voice recorder, video, and camera on their cell phone, everyone in leadership should be extremely cautious. One public display of verbal overflow could last a decade. When we serve in a public office or in leadership, people hold us to a higher standard, and we should rise to this standard. Therefore, never use low empathy with a subordinate, a business associate, or loved one during any meaningful conversation.

Medium Empathy—Speaking to Listen

Medium empathy is neither expounding nor uncaring; these words are always in the middle, calmer, and are always clarifying, or pointing the conversation in a positive direction. Therefore, to win at Verbal Chess, we don't consistently engage in high empathy or low empathy but a balance between the two—we call "medium empathy." This is "My goal . . . that they may be encouraged in heart and united in compassion, so that they may have the full riches of complete understanding . . ."[77] Medium empathy is not only the words we speak but the underlying silent message we communicate. It is the key to understanding many of the inner-most thoughts of another.

Medium empathy necessitates and encourages a response from the opponent. It is speaking to listen. Medium empathy can also be used to subtly direct or point the conversation to a desired area. It shows interest and understanding: the Royalty of Verbal Chess. Medium empathy also helps to diffuse hostility and drain information from our opponent so we can strategize on the best way to proceed.

Consider the simple example of somebody telling us, "It's raining outside." Medium empathy rephrases the question and asks, "Is it really raining?" Then the person who made the initial statement is compelled to speak. This is a key to medium empathy. It is speaking to enable us to use the Bishop of Verbal Chess to listen with our ears and eyes.

Remember the story about my daughter who I heard advising my younger daughter to count the gray hairs on my head? I followed up and asked her out to breakfast. Before we went out the next morning, she went to a couple of her sisters and even talked to Mom asking, "What does Dad want?"

What I wanted was to have a conversation to allow me to gain a better relationship with her. We met at the restaurant, and I asked her what she would like. She ordered and it was obvious she was a little intimidated and didn't want to say much. She probably thought Dad was going to give her another lecture or something. Sometimes in Verbal Chess it is very important to start the conversation with a short story using a medium empathy statement. This is a natural process because all humans are social creatures by nature, and most want to be heard.

I was not completely sure at that moment what kind of a short story would prompt my daughter to speak. So, I said, "The other day I was going through a parking lot in the mall, and I came within inches of a person running into the side to me." This story was only fifteen to twenty words long. My daughter looked up at me, I could see she was thinking, and she then told me her story. She told me how at college the other day, she was walking out of the parking lot when a young student driving "a piece of junk," according to her, came barreling by and she thought he was going to hit her. It was then I started using medium empathy paraphrasing, which in this case is rephrasing her question, "You almost got hit?" This compels others to speak. She verbally took off telling me not only about the incident, but how the college needs to put in some speed bumps. Later in this conversation, I wanted to find out how she is doing in her classes, so I directed the conversation by asking, "What classes do you like best?" She expounded on her classes and told me she was doing very well and mentioned her boyfriend who shares a class with her. What father of daughters doesn't want to know about a new boyfriend? So, I asked, "What is he majoring in?" Again, she took off, telling me everything about him. I started asking two- or three-word questions, "How tall?" She expounds even more. Then I wanted to direct the conversation to his upbringing and because I had already used these short questions many times, she was used to them. So, I asked, "His parents?" She started telling me his dad was a doctor and his mother a homemaker.

Notice these short rephrasings or paraphrasings are calm questions that do not raise doubt or suggest ulterior motives. Our opponent, in this case my daughter, readily answered them. Then

I wanted to change the focus and I asked, "Your birthday?" She started telling me everything she wanted for her birthday, and what she was planning, etc. It was a great time; my daughter was affirmed by her father, and I got a long hug before she left and the statement, "Let's do this again."

Redirecting the Conversation

Let's use another simple example. Let's say an employee says, "This organization is the lousiest organization. I've tried to get my payroll check for two weeks and they still have not sent it." We might rephrase by saying, "You didn't get your check?" Again, they will be compelled to explain and say something like, "I think they are doing this on purpose." We say, "They are doing it on purpose?" They are again compelled to speak and define their allegation, which can work to substantiate or defeat it.

Paraphrasing is to gain better understanding of a real problem or the point others are trying to define. This also empowers us to redirect the conversation to the area we want to know more about. Learning to paraphrase by rephrasing the question takes a little patience, but it is interesting how much information we can obtain. It starts to be fun because we ask questions without the opponent even knowing, and they are feeling affirmed. We then gain control over the conversation by directing instead of being directed. A caution: use the Bishop to listen with our eyes and ears to keep us from using too much paraphrasing.

Medium empathy, as I've related, necessitates and encourages a response from your opponent. This is why my daughter had to respond to my short story. It causes us to want to talk back. If we use it subtly to direct the conversation to the area desired, it makes a great sales and interviewing technique. When we are interviewing people, like I have for years, we want to be able to get certain information. People who are being interviewed are not necessarily going to want to give information. They are reluctant to tell certain things because they have friendships, reasons, or maybe biases that prevent them from wanting to open up.

Once they start talking, we can start directing the conversation and start getting information. They will not even realize they have told us the things we want them to expound upon. Once we get people talking, it is like opening the door. To do this successfully we must show interest, understanding, and most of all give them the Queen's grace and never stop listening with our eyes and ears.

This technique can diffuse hostility and drain information from an opponent while they are being affirmed. This is our goal because the more information we can drain out of our opponent the better decisions we can make based on that information.

The technique is simply inserting the third person into the two-person dialogue to say their meaning in our words. We cast the real point of their words in our own words, then we insert a new idea phrase that directs and clarifies the conversation. These are calm words because they are affirming. They enable us to direct and clarify so we can be sure we heard the other person correctly, and now they know we are listening. Suddenly, we do not have their words with their meaning, we have our words speaking their meaning. These words are always clarifying, calming, or pointing to the area we want to explore, like the boyfriend questions above.

This is one of the most powerful tools in communication. We are speaking to understand and controlling the direction of the conversation to obtain as much information as possible before it is our turn to speak, intelligently.

Using medium empathy enables people to start speaking about difficult issues. Most humans like to talk, and medium empathy starts them, opens the door, and gives them an excuse, setting them in verbal motion. Once we start the verbal motion, we are off to the races, so to speak. Medium empathy paraphrasing lets us set limits and boundaries, and enables us to have the chance to hear, see, and read our opponent's innermost feelings.

A good example is when a loved one, associate, employee, friend, coworker, etc., says, "I would like to talk." This usually means they want to have a serious or important conversation. To show we are going to listen, make a pronounced movement. Ask them to sit down where there is no barrier such as a table or desk. If we are wearing glasses reach up and remove our glasses and then invite them to sit down. Likewise, if we are wearing a hat, take it off. Men, if you have a remote control in your hand, shut off the TV and put the remote down. All of this is telling the loved one, associate, employee etc., that we respect them and want to take the time to speak to them. Moreover, it tells them we are going to listen empathetically. It is at this point, while we are preparing to listen, we watch the person's body language, and control our own.

Intense Encounters

The more intense the encounter, the more critically important it is to slow down. We need to show empathy: if somebody is excited, slowing down allows empathy to rise up and influence. Without slowing, our emotions will stay heightened. However, if we can get our own emotions to slow down, we can gain mind, mouth, and body control. We are also slowing them down if they are excited and using verbal overflow. We are hearing them accurately explain themselves and, if angry, with less emotion.

The Knight: Strategic Speaking

Our opponent in Verbal Chess is now a better listener because we are rephrasing their words into our words. This inserts calm and reason into the emotional situation. Now we are in the game and we are playing to win. We are not dealing with an explosive situation, because the persona of the King and the grace of the Queen give us the opportunity to edify and gain the trust of the person we are speaking to.

Emotional Dementia—Speaking to Listen

Paraphrasing overcomes a strange phenomenon I call "emotional dementia." When people are in an emotional or angry confrontation, they often think they have said something they did not say. Heightened emotion can cause all kinds of strange responses. It could be our opponent rehearsed what they were going to say and thought they had said it. If people are emotional and think they said something during a confrontation, often no amount of argument or evidence can change their minds. If we try to convince them that they did not say whatever, the argument can then gravitate to even more confrontation. This is where the Royalty, especially giving the Queen's grace, is needed. My advice is: do not react; just move around them with the Knight of Verbal Chess and keep on going. This is not the time to argue over how or what was said. This is the time to be an empathic and attentive listener.

What if we have two people in a conversation and neither one of them is practicing Verbal Chess? They are practicing verbal combat, and this is leading to some kind of confrontation. We realize we must mediate, and it's only through paraphrasing, asking calm questions, that we will have a chance of getting them to listen. Also, it depends on how long the verbal combat has gone on. If we are in authority, we can certainly say, "Okay, wait a minute. I want to tell you both that no one is listening. Why don't we move over here, and sit down and talk this out?" When we move them, we are essentially extracting them from the situation they have placed themselves in (the Castle of Verbal Chess). It is then we start asking questions through paraphrasing their points to get them to verbally expound on the problem they are facing.

Let's say this is unsuccessful. Our next option is to cut this argument short and have a timeout. Many times this is the only way we are going to get them to shut down verbal combat and turn the heat down. We do the same thing with little children and teenagers. We separate them, let them calm down, and then agree on a time to come back together and discuss the conflict.

Strategic Medium Empathy Questions

We can use strategic medium empathy questions to compel the opponent to listen. This is a good technique if we have a boss, spouse, children, etc., who will not listen.

I worked for a very large company in California and had a boss who did not listen. So, I decided to use preplanned medium empathy questions that showed he was the solution. Over a cup of coffee during a break I told him I was having a hard time talking to him because I didn't seem to be able to make my point or explain it in a way that he could understand. (Notice, I was the problem. This is giving the Queen's grace to gain understanding.)

He said, "Well, when we are through why don't you come to my office and we will discuss this?" After we sat down in his office, I said, "George, if it's okay with you, can I tell you the whole story, and then please, can you give me your comments?" I asked to set the ground rules and he listened because he wanted to know how he could help. He said, "That's great." I continued with problem.

This type of process or technique obtains people's undivided attention because we are speaking to get them to speak, so they must listen. This was the only way I was able to get this boss to listen to me. This works like magic with spouses, teenage children, co-workers, who will not listen.

I have also used another technique with a non-listening boss: I put my concerns or ideas in memo form, then requested them to reply in written form. None of them ever wanted to respond in writing. They have always called me and listened to the point of the memo. This opened the door for the use of a lot of medium empathy paraphrasing to create meaningful conversation using Verbal Chess with people who do not listen naturally.

Reverse Paraphrasing

Reverse paraphrasing is used to make sure that we have heard the other person correctly. It's interesting, studies show eight of ten people misunderstand most normal verbal exchanges. Reverse paraphrasing is asking people to duplicate what they said, or it is asking them to repeat what they said. We could say something like this: "To make sure I understood you correctly, could you tell me that again." Or we could say, "What I'm hearing you say is . . ." then we tell them what we thought they said. We should never forget in a verbal exchange *the responsibility for understanding is on the speaker not on the listener*. Reverse paraphrasing makes us empathetic and ensures a clear understanding. This is where we speak to listen and gain understanding. To paraphrase back makes us empathetic and ensures a clear understanding. It creates a win-win and that is the whole purpose of Verbal Chess: to create a winning strategy.

Speaking on the Phone

When talking on the cell phone, from a listener's point of view, there are two elements, which carry the most weight. Content and voice is the only thing people hear. Content carries about ten percent of the weight, which is saying words only carry about ten percent of others' understanding. Voice or tone carries the weight of about ninety percent of the understanding. Voice is in the tone and pitch, which is how we are saying it. It shows if we are tired, not really concerned, upset, happy, etc. Our vocal tone and pitch are going to come through loud and clear. How we say it is more important than what we say.

People who conduct sales calls know it is more important how they say something than what they say. When the voice is right, people want to listen. Contrast that with picking up the phone and someone is borderline rude, and they don't even pronounce the rehearsed words correctly; we realize they are from another country. How fast do we hang up? Our voice is our verbal personality as heard by the other person. Tone can be a deadly four-letter word. Why is tone so important? What is the oldest phrase in the world? I think it might be, *I love you*. What if I say, "I love you!" passionately? It means I love you. Let's change the tone. I'm going to say, "I love you?" but this time I'm going to change the modulation put a little extra lift on the word, *you*. I turn the statement into a question. In English we can do this with almost any phrase. Another example is "I'm really concerned about how your day is going," versus emphasizing certain words, changing the rhythm, and pausing making this phrase sound like I'm not concerned at all.

Tone has three elements: pace, pitch, and modulation. Pace is speed, and pitch is how high or how low. Have we ever talked to someone who has one of those high squeaky voices? It's very hard to want to continue to talk to them. Modulation is your rhythm, and this plays a big part.

Tone and modulation are so powerful because they convey your attitude towards people, your *real* attitude. If we want to calm people, the modulation of our voice has to be such that it assures them. "Please, it's going to be okay." The key is, when we are speaking, no matter what we say, we need to say it with sincere medium empathy. Where does medium empathy come from? It comes from the persona of the King and is expressed through giving the Queen's grace. Through this we are able to gain an insight into others' feelings, whether they are kind, exploiting, or condemning. We must step back and see them and the situation as they truly are, maintaining our sincerity throughout.

Let me repeat this: no matter what we say, if we say it with sincere medium empathy, we will be perceived as being concerned. We need to remember, once we trust in medium empathy, we can influence a difficult opponent. Many times we can get them to comply voluntarily. We will begin to see them as an interesting challenge or opportunity rather than as an obstacle. For most of my life I've looked at difficult people and all I wanted to do was what my grandma said, "Give them a good letting alone." If I never talked to them again it would be too soon. But now, having learned the Christian Art of Verbal Chess, I see difficult people as a challenge.

Let me give you an example of a difficult situation in my life where I put all the traits of the Bishop into practice. Saying the wrong thing could have put me in the hospital. During the Gray Lord investigation in Chicago, where a number of Chicago attorneys were paying off judges, I volunteered to be one of the first agents to act like a private citizen and get arrested for drunk driving. The FBI arranged and I volunteered to get arrested for drunk driving under an assumed name, so I could hire one of those attorneys and provide the money to pay off the judge.

We decided to do this on the south side of Chicago. I dressed up like a working man and poured some booze on my clothes and on the seat of the car. I spotted two unsuspecting police officers and started driving erratically. I ran a red light and immediately got pulled over. Both of these officers were very professional and, of course I was very polite. They arrested me for drunk driving, took me to the station and the desk sergeant gave me the opportunity to make a phone call. I called a special number to talk to another agent who was supposed to come and bail me out within an hour.

The desk sergeant decided not to let the other FBI agents, who had disguised themselves as my friends, pick me up. He placed me in a jail cell with eight other individuals, all black, who had been arrested that evening. As I was waiting in the cell things started getting tense. The looks of anger I was getting, and the comments were threatening. Since I was still standing next to the jail cell door, I scanned the room trying to find a friendly face. There was an older gentleman who was not participating, sitting in the corner by himself and he had *Simper Fi* tattooed on his arm, meaning always faithful. I walked over and sat next to him and asked, "Were you in the Marines?" He was half drunk, opened one eye, and said, "What is it to you?" I told a short story. I'd served in the Army during the Vietnam conflict and my best friend Bruce Patterson was a Marine who was killed in 1967. I continued with how Bruce and I played football together in 1963. He then told me that he played quarterback in high school. I was answering him with another paraphrased question when another guy walked over, stood in front of me, and told me to "Shut the %&@! up." Another piped up and said, "I don't want to hear this asshole talk."

The Knight: Strategic Speaking

I tried not to look at anyone, and kept my head staring straight ahead. I realized I might be pushing the envelope, but I asked the ex-Marine, "Where did you serve?"

While he started telling me about his time in Vietnam another guy in the jail cell said, "I thought we told you to shut the %&@! up," indicating me. The ex-Marine said nonchalantly, "I'm talking to him," and didn't say anything further. We continued conversing and my stomach was starting to burn from the fear. Many more times I was verbally challenged and threatened but the ex-Marine paid no attention and just kept talking to me, and I did the same.

I believe this ex-Marine was my salvation. After three long hours, the desk sergeant opened the jail cell and accused all of those in the cell of "being a bunch of pussys," because they didn't beat the living hell out of me. He disgustedly told me to come out, and I walked into the outer room where the FBI agent who was to pick me up was waiting. The desk sergeant again berated me, called me white ass honky, but let me leave. I got into the car with the other FBI agent, and he said, "We were really getting worried." I said, "I think I am going to throw up." My stomach had been burning for three hours. He said, "Hold on, let's get out of the south side." He was taking me home, so I asked him to stop at a Burger King or something. We stopped in about ten minutes. My stomach was starting to calm down and we stopped. So, I purchased a milk shake to put the fire out. It was one of the scariest three hours of my life.

I believe to this day that controlling my fear and searching for someone who had something in common with me, helped me a great deal. Plus, using the short story to start the conversation, not showing any aggressive body language or using any low empathy statements, combined with not addressing the threats while talking to the ex-Marine, saved my bacon.

8

The Castle

SILENT COMMUNICATION

THE LYRICS OF the old song "The Sound of Silence" says: "The vision that was planted in my brain still remains, within the sound of silence." It is "people talking without speaking, people hearing without listening"[78] This is the sound of silent communication all humans project every moment they are awake. When we really look at others, we get a vision in our brains of what they are silently saying; we hear people speak through their silent language. I cannot overstate how important it is to know and read silent communication.

Understanding the sounds of silent communication and controlling our own silent communication is necessary to clearly speak life into others. It is like hearing the spirit or melody of a song, but through the melody we know the true meaning is bigger and more important than the words. This is the sound of silence, of our silent body language and the opponent's.

Body language can be a key to success in both personal and professional relationships. When we communicate well, it is not the words we use but our nonverbal cues or "body language" that speaks the loudest like the beat in the melody.

The Castle: Silent Communication

Our silent language contains three important aspects that encompass sixty percent of communication: reading the other person's body language (their melody), then controlling our body language (our melody), and then controlling the distance from each other while the melody beats and we speak words. This is watching and reading the body movement of another while they speak and being able to control our body language while using personal space to enhance the message we are trying to convey.

The true benefit of reading silent communication is understanding what is *not* being said, combined with listening to what *is* being said. This is to understand, "Even fools are thought wise if they keep silent, and discerning if they hold their tongues."[79] However, even fools unfold what is unsaid through their body language. This leads us to discover the hidden truth of what was not said.

Silent communication, the Castle of Verbal Chess, as represented in this book, is not meant to make you an expert at reading body language. To be an expert at body language takes intense training and years of practice. However, the Castle of Verbal Chess is designed to make us better at observing other people's silent language and mastering our own.

Master Communicators do not have to be experts at understanding all the details of body language. However, we have to be masters of the total countenance of what people are silently projecting. Learning this we will be able to answer questions like: is our opponent afraid, self-concerned, sad, violent, depressed, or angry, etc.? Detecting these general attitudes during meaningful communication is critical during meaningful communication.

When we are having a meaningful conversation using Verbal Chess this observant skill will enable us to be an inflow enabler and a strategic outflow expert. Master observers know how to detect and notice changes in people's body language which greatly assists them in understanding and being able to respond to the opponent of Verbal Chess.

The silent language is truly another kind of listening that will reveal wonders upon wonders about the person we are communicating with. This power of observation, once learned, is addicting, and we will never want to lose it. This is understanding *as much as is possible* through seeing others' body language and controlling our own, giving us the wisdom to strategically communicate at the right distance.

Once we grasp the concept, we begin to discover the truth about other people. It enables us to greatly influence the conversation by being able to heat it up and cool it off through controlling the distance from which we communicate.

The Castle is our silent vehicle of communication to understand what is not spoken and influences our opponent covertly. It also moves forward and backward, side-to-side, changing the playing field by presenting different views of our inner self and outward demeanor.

Body Language is Our Physical Behavior

Body language includes expressions and mannerisms that communicate nonverbally. Our mannerisms are often instinctive rather than conscious, which is why it is important to read and be in command of our own body language.

There are generally five ways body language is displayed:

- Friendly nonaggressive body language
- Withdrawal body leverage
- Defensive body language
- Aggressive body language
- Unusual mannerisms

To read body language we must:

FIRST, scan from head to toe. Always be able to see the whole person, looking for clues during the development of rapport.

SECOND, do not judge a book by its cover, but look for telling clues (distractions, outward signs, etc.).

THIRD, look for consistent changes in normal mannerisms.

FOURTH, exercise caution. Inappropriate or unusual mannerisms deserve special attention.

FIFTH, keep command of your own body language to influence your opponent/client.

SIXTH, communicate in the appropriate personal zone.

We don't need to be experts at reading body language, but we need to learn to be proficient at watching the body language of others and controlling our own. This is being completely aware of our opponent's body language and how we are projecting ours. The biggest, bestselling book ever, written a couple of thousand years ago, says, "Body language can expose a person's intentions . . ."[80] This is totally true, and we want to be able to expose a person's intentions as we involve ourselves in meaningful communication.

Body language includes our face and eyes, hands and arms, and legs and feet. The parts of the body we have the most control over are first, face and eyes; second, hands and arms; and third, legs and feet. It is very important for us to understand this because we have the least control over our legs and feet. Keeping watch over the movement of legs and feet gives us intelligence. Someone could say they were not nervous but have nervous leg movements. Facial expressions, our countenance, we have learned almost from birth how to change to try to mirror how we want to look.

Facial expressions are extremely expressive, able to convey countless emotions without saying a word. They are also able to hide feelings for personal or illicit purposes. The eyes and mouth are especially important in facial expressions because they can quickly change, and the change can tell us a lot. We should always pay attention to immediate changes, noting transitions that are not consistent. I will repeat this several times, because inconsistencies and unusual mannerisms can reveal the true motives behind the rest of the body's actions.

Body language generally mirrors our mindset, such as: dishonesty, irritation, anger, honesty, happiness, joy, concern, alarm, and surprise, to name just a few. We learn in watching and trying to read body language that when people are truthful, they look comfortable and express positive body language. When a person is unhappy or lying, they display negative body language. Generally, dishonesty and anger are displayed negatively while honesty and happiness are displayed in positive ways. However, negative body language is always harder to read than positive body language. The reason is we are glad to express honesty, but we learn to mask dishonesty.

A good example of this is when I discovered my six-year-old grandson in the kitchen at 7 a.m. pilfering cookies. When I walked around the corner, he was standing looking at me with both arms behind his back, obviously holding something like a cookie, swaying back and forth, with a big smile on his face. He was so cute and clever, but how do you think he learned this body language? No one taught him.

The Book of Truth says, "... whoever winks the eye is planning perversity; whoever purses his lips is intent on evil."[81] This is true. The point is a person's intentions can be revealed in the way they control or fail to control their facial expressions, combined with the rest of their body language. A wink to another is an understanding not spoken. A purse of the lips is unspoken dissatisfaction.

If we really want to know what a particularly unusual mannerism or body language means, sit or stand looking in a mirror and repeat the mannerism. This is the best way I know to understand someone's unusual body language or mannerisms. The key is, we must see and concentrate on the unspoken language to gain insight in order to win at Verbal Chess. We don't have to totally understand everything about other people's body language, we just have to be aware of it. However, not learning to see and question body language means we "... may be ever seeing but never perceiving, and ... never understanding."[82]

Developing a Baseline of Truthful Responses

The baseline technique is only used when we are having a meaningful conversation. It is not meant to be a tactic when we have a casual or friendly conversation. Therefore, a baseline of truthful body language responses is obtained when we converse with people in a meaningful way. This is a critical step in which we discover a person's natural use of body language. When a person is sitting or standing in front of us, we start conversing with them while watching how they use their silent language. We may start with asking questions about subjects that can be honestly answered. These subjects range from hobbies, family, to background, etc.

If we know someone is into a sport or some type of cooking, we can ask them about these subjects where we will get truthful responses. This usually happens at the beginning of a meaningful conversation, but because of other reasons, we may want to use the baseline questions during the conversation.

To recap, in developing a baseline of mannerisms, we are looking for the person's normal body language, while they are telling us a truthful story. Let me give another example. If we strike up a conversation with a person who likes football, as he describes the game and the teams, his body language will show normal truthful responses. This will be the baseline we are looking for as we continue the conversation.

Then as we get into the interview or conversation, we receive explanations or start hearing answers we can judge against the person's baseline of responses. These are responses to the more important, or possibly controversial issues.

When we talked about football, the person's face was relaxed, neither happy nor sad, their body was leaning a little forward in their chair displaying interest, and they were using positive hand gestures to make the points. We can conclude we have a good idea of their truthful responses.

We note these truthful body language responses in our memory, or even record them in our notes. We then compare them with this person's body language as they are answering questioning about an incident, or situation. Now while they are explaining an incident, we note the transition in body language. They are now leaning back in their chair, at times covering their mouths with their hands, and occasionally grooming themselves.

Most body language is easy to decipher when we think about it. Sitting back could be withdrawing or moving away, covering their mouth is a form of covering up, and grooming themselves is self-concern. This is not rocket science. This is a plain indication we may not be getting truthful responses, or the person is very concerned. Their mannerisms have changed from the baseline of truthful responses to withdrawal, covering up, and self-concern, and this has alerted us that we need further discovery to explain the changes.

Now this is important: body language is helpful in understanding a person's truthfulness but it's not a panacea or an absolute. We have to review the conversation in its entirety to draw conclusions but mastering the ability to observe will certainly give us a tremendous amount of information we would not normally have.

Let me explain a personal experience of unusual body language which turned out to indicate total truthfulness. As an FBI agent in Chicago, we had a monthly duty to cover walk-ins. A man came in and said he had knowledge of political corruption. We went into a small office, and I tried to get him to talk about himself, but he was so nervous he just had to spill out the information.

I consented, but every time he got to an important fact, he would turn his head to the right and look at the wall while he was speaking. Now this went on for at least thirty minutes. I left the room, got him something to drink, and came back with a voice recorder. I started again to obtain his recorded statement. Again, he did exactly the same thing. Every time he told me about a fact or an incident, he turned his head to the right, faced the wall, and responded.

After the interview, I decided to try to get a baseline of truthful responses because frankly, I had never seen this before. I asked him if he was an NFL, Chicago Bears fan. He looked at me with a smile and told me about the many years he had been a Bears fan. Every time he got to an important fact about a player or a past game, he would turn his head to the right, face the wall, and respond. This was most amazing, but he was being totally truthful.

This is why it is critical to gain a baseline of truthful body language responses or we will not be able to gage the truthfulness of the person we are conversing with.

The Face and Eyes

It has been said the face has more expressions than the stars in the sky. Here is the short list: happiness, sadness, anger, embarrassment, exhaustion, confusion, contempt, humility, seduction, smugness, arrogance, pleasure, frustration, boredom, shame, astonishment, dismay, focus, surprise, gloom, and disgust. If we zero in on just the eyes and the essential part they play in the display of emotions, we can see how a person can accent or blur every one of these facial expressions.

Studies have shown humans have the most control over the face because it is closest to the brain. We have less control over the hands and arms and many times no control over our legs and feet. However, humans learn to conceal their feelings by controlling facial expressions almost from birth, as the little boy with the cookies. We can show deceptive facial expression instead of how we truly feel almost at will. This is done for numerous reasons, from trying not to offend to attempting to scam someone out of something.

On-Time Transitions and Micro expressions

Reading facial expressions can be difficult but there are certain observations that can give the body language reader insight or an edge. This is the skill of noticing on-time micro expressions, which happen momentarily in a microsecond—a transition from one facial expression to another.

A micro expression is a brief, involuntary display which appears on a person's face according to the emotions being experienced. Unlike regular, pro-longed facial expressions, it is difficult to fake a micro expression. Therefore, the masters of Verbal Chess must watch and listen very carefully. There are normally seven micro expressions: surprise, disgust, anger, fear, sadness, happiness, and contempt—all which can start and change in a microsecond. Deciphering the meaning of micro facial expressions is difficult but achievable.

Here is a hypothetical example. A young man comes to the door to talk to a young woman who he has upset. He has planned a made-up excuse that involves trying to make himself look better than he really is. She comes to the door with a frown on her face. He starts his explanation, and she is obviously not believing it because suddenly her eyes narrow almost into a squint. He fails to see this because he is so concerned about himself. This probably means she is trying to figure him out. Then her face turns to a kind of disgust, and then her head slightly leans to the left, like saying, "Really?!"

The next micro transition takes place: while he is still speaking, from the corner of her mouth she starts to crack a smile. He missed the eyes, the disgust, but sees the crack of a smile and thinks he is pulling one over on her. She realizes he is buying her false smile, because he smiles, looks down, and puts his hands in his pockets. She reads this as insincerity and proceeds with a wider friendlier smile, and even nods her head as if she is believing him. She is really saying to herself, *you think I'm an idiot*. He continues to smile, convinced that he has pulled it off. When he finishes, he pauses, and asks her if she will forgive him. On-time she goes from smiling big, and quickly transitions to a malicious frown, and says, "Not in your lifetime!" and slams the door.

If the young man first would have had the persona of the Royalty of Verbal Chess, he would not have tried to lie his way through an apology. Apologies, when sincere, display remorseful body language. Also, had he been knowledgeable of on-time micro facial changes and paid better attention, he may have had a chance of mending this relationship with the knowledge that she was not buying it. Instead he made himself look bad.

Much of what this young man missed was caused by trying to sell her a whopper and focusing on his own performance. He did not have any idea how he was doing because he missed interpreting the transitions. He should have realized she was not buying his baloney but at that point, he had already lost the game of Verbal Chess. The transition was from a normal look to a surprised look. She did not need to say what she was really thinking; any observant listener would have known.

The Master Communicator can use information the opponent doesn't know the interviewer knows and bait them with it to see if they can obtain a micro transition. This is done simply to get an on-time micro expression, an involuntary facial expression, from the person being interviewed to determine previous knowledge or to ascertain if they are lying.

When I was in the FBI in Chicago, I was interviewing an electrical inspector I believed was taking bribes, which is political corruption. During the baseline development stage, he kept his face in a natural, unemotional expression. He exhibited total control and was a polished liar. He did not know I had conducted a thorough background on him before the interview. Plus, my expectations were to determine how he was going to lie to me. He was of course denying involvement, so I baited him to see if I could get an on-time surprised look. The surprised look would confirm my suspicions or, at the very least, worry him.

We had previously discussed his salary in this interview. At this time he was making about thirty thousand dollars a year. He pompously agreed that if electrical inspectors were taking bribes, they would purchase expensive things like cars. He kept his face within the baseline of lying, without much emotion.

Then, I leaned over closer, looking him in the eyes, moving into his intimate zone which we will discuss later, and said, "You own two Mercedes-Benz sedans; one is your wife's and the other is yours." His involuntary surprised look appeared just for a microsecond, on-time. He very quickly got control and returned to his baseline lying look. This accomplished identifying this fellow as a liar, and the investigation continued successfully.

Truism: what we should all take away from this is honest people don't lie. They may have a surprised look in these kinds of situations, but most will immediately dispute the information and offer proof.

Mixed Messages

When people give off mixed messages, they often are not wanting to confront or correct us. There are other times when mixed messages can alert us to life-threating situations.

Let's recall the story of the sales meeting when my employee controlled the conversation. While my employee was dominating the conversation and enjoying his own stories about hunting, the CEO was sitting behind his desk with a half-smile on his face. His eyes opened a little wider, and he was massaging his pen in a nervous manner. The CEO then transitioned to start tapping his fingers on his pen. Next, he transitioned to leaning back in his chair (withdrawing). A few seconds later, he was using his pen like a small hammer hitting his desk showing obvious impatience for all the world to see. This made no difference to my employee. He was so engrossed in his own conversation he did not know what was going on with the person he was talking to. We should all take note: failing at the Christian Art of Verbal Chess is having a self-serving, self-edifying conversation.

When we first meet a person, just because they are smiling doesn't mean they are not harboring deceit, or violence. People commonly use a smile to disarm us and give us a feeling of peace. Salespeople do this all the time. However, what if their mixed message could be an attempt to do us wrong?

While an FBI agent in Chicago, I was covering leads for another FBI office. They were looking for a fugitive who had killed a police officer in a mall restroom. The police officer, after he had received a report that a man with a gun had entered the restroom at a mall went in to check it out. The officer had limited information and he did not have a complete description. In reading the report, I was shocked by what the officer said to the first responders after he was shot. He told them several times as they were trying to stop the bleeding, "He was smiling, he was smiling!" Later, before he passed away, he told the investigator that the killer never took his eyes off him and had a smile on his face. A truism about evil,

> The eye is the lamp of the body. So, if your eye is healthy, your whole body will be full of light, but if your eye is bad, your whole body will be full of darkness. If then the light in you is darkness, how great is the darkness![83]

The Castle: Silent Communication

How great was this darkness? It killed the police officer, not to mention the murderous effect it had on the life of his wife and children who grieved for the rest of their lives.

What mixed message did the killer exhibit? The mixed message was missed because the police officer was watching the killer's face and eyes, not his hands. Could the killer have been smiling to disarm the police officer and make himself look less threatening? The answer is yes! If we are threatened by someone, we don't just watch their face, because the face cannot hurt us. What will hurt us is in their hands.

There are many instances where victims of sociopaths—who lived to tell about it—commented on how the sociopath stared at them. Some women have even mentioned at first, they thought it was sexy. Later, after they found out the guy was a psychopath, they would remark how they had never seen eyes like that before: pure evil. Could the realization this man was a sociopath have been evident if these women would have watched and tried to decipher all the sociopath's body language, instead of just his face? Could the sociopath have sent false messages? Could the victims have drawn a baseline of untruthful responses? Like with the sociopath I interviewed in jail who was so engaging the hair stood up on my back, I believe the answer is yes.

Sociopaths depend on convincing people of their lies, and when we are young, wanting attention, our longings often overcome our good sense. I believe teaching young people to watch the body language of people they don't know could keep many of them from becoming victims—if they will act on their conclusions.

Like animals on the hunt, predators never take their eyes off their victims. A personal example was when I lived near Santa Rosa, California. My family and I went to a big flea market. I separated from my wife, her mother, and my daughters to look for guy things. I kept watch over them by looking up occasionally. Twice when I looked up the same man was following my wife and family. His body and his face were facing the back of my wife. When my eyes moved to my wife, I could see she was carrying her purse over her shoulder on her back with a long strap, making her purse easy to grab. I quickly started moving towards her to intercept him. Then at the last second, before, I believe, he was going to steal her purse, he turned and scanned the crowd looking for security. He immediately noticed me staring at him and coming towards him. He turned and fled. My wife was his target, and he was mine. He never hesitated when he saw me, because he could tell by my eyes that his illicit game had been discovered.

It has been proven over the years that criminals who prey on people focus intently on their victims. He is just like a deer hunter who never takes his eyes off the deer for fear that he may not see the deer again. Predators hope for victims who are not aware of their surroundings, just like a lion picks out an unaware gazelle. This is important for everyone to consider, but especially women. When we are alone, like in a parking lot, we must keep track of the people around us to protect ourselves. Most human predators do not want to be noticed, because they want to surprise their victims. The key to avoid being a victim is to stay aware of our surroundings.

To recap, how important is the face when looking at the whole picture including the hands, arms, body, legs, and feet? The face is the readily changeable vehicle of the body, but the whole body gives us the complete picture. The face and eyes can be a giveaway, or an enticement. Watching the whole body is a must if we want to understand a person's silent language.

Hands and Arms

Hand and arm positioning is one of the biggest clues to someone's thoughts and emotions along with the face and eyes. The arms and hands are further from the brain and, from my experience, are more spontaneously truthful than the face. When someone is happy, they will move their hands and arms in an animated manner, like someone describing the final catch that won the Super Bowl. The opposite is a person who is feeling down or is in mourning. Their arms hang down heavily, thus depicting their mood.

Most of us use our hands and arms to gesticulate when we speak. Adults, however, learn to conceal their emotions with their face. When we watch adults argue they lose their inhibitions (self-control) and start getting excited and hand and arm movements become more animated.

Hand movements are also used to mimic the words being said by self—mirroring or replaying the event. For example, if a person who recently went shooting, is telling another person about the great shot they made, his fingers may look like a gun as he is describing the fantastic shot.

Hands and arms definitely give off some signals that need to be seen. When people are told about an incident they disagree with or dislike they tend to pull their hands closer to their bodies. When they are concentrating, they may steeple their fingers. When people are self-conscious, they may groom themselves. When they are amazed or shocked, sometimes they put their fingers over their mouth. Or in the case of the rapist I was interviewing, he started putting his hands on top of his legs and rubbing them when he was getting sexually excited.

When a person is pointing his finger at us, this is a threatening gesture. Never, never get into a conversation with somebody and start pointing your finger at them because this destroys the conversation. The person we are pointing at can literally feel it and this gives them the opportunity to be upset.

Try this test on someone. Tell them you are going to show them something and are wondering if they can feel it even if you do not touch them. Get them ready, and then point your finger at them and add a little drama like making your face look mean. Over ninety percent of the attendees in my classes over the years have said they could feel it.

Then try a different approach. Try the same experiment, but use an open hand pointing all four fingers. People don't feel a thing, but they know we are trying to make a point. Therefore, if you must make a point, open your hand and point all of your fingers.

When we are speaking truthfully, we may use palm gestures. Remember the old cowboy and Indian movies with the Indian holding his hand up showing his palm and saying, "How?" This palm gesture evidently shows no ill intent. However, it seems that if the speaker believes the truth of what they are saying is obvious and readily accepted, they most likely will not use a palms up gesture. Conversely, when a salesman is trying to convince us the item is as cheap as they can go, the salesman may be using the palms up gesture to convince us he is telling the truth.

A word of caution: When people mix body languages, unusual mannerisms, which may be truthful and untruthful at the same time, this can be deceptive or threatening. Take note and beware something is not right. Most truthful people, who have no ulterior motive, do not use aggressive gestures like finger pointing when they are being truthful. In other words, people do not point, or show a fist, when they are trying to truthfully explain something.

The Castle: Silent Communication

A great example of mixed messages was a past president who on national TV said, "I never had sexual relations with that woman!" Remember him? He was pointing his finger at the listeners while his face displayed a stern look saying, "I never had relations with that woman!" When I saw this, I started calling my wife from the other room saying, "Honey, please come quick! The president is lying through his teeth." And he was!

Normally, we show honest gestures with a look of concern on our face. We don't act like the congressman who was accused of public corruption: while he was trying to claim his innocence, he held his arms out straight showing his palms. He was waving his arms like he was going to take off. This is not an honest gesture.

He was trying to display honesty, but just could not get it done. This was truly a mixed message. However, when we do show honest palm gestures our arms are normally out in front of us. This language is more a pleading motion, while showing our palms, and is truthful.

Other arm gestures we may notice are arms behind the back, or arms akimbo, which are arms bent and hands on our hips. Arms behind our back can mean confidence or hiding something. Arms akimbo generally indicates a combination of impatience and defiance. When people's arms are crossed over their chest with their hands wrapped under their opposite arm, they are normally closed off to hearing anything, or busy protecting themselves. If a person's arms are swinging to the front and back along their side, this can mean aggression. The key again is to watch how people transition from one body language to another.

Legs and Feet

When it comes to nonverbal body language, legs and feet are the parts of our body we have the least control over. When we are standing with our feet about the width of our shoulders, this shows we are relaxed. If our legs are slightly wider, this indicates we are feeling confident. Then if our feet are a little bit wider still, this can be a signal of power and dominance. This dominant pose takes up more space. It can also signal that we are ready for another person's attack. When one foot is forward and the other is slightly behind this can show we are taking an extra stable position in case of frontal attack. This is used in martial arts.

Another aggressive stance is when a person stands with legs apart in an aggressive way and rotates up on to the balls of their feet showing height. This is really accented if they move their arms and hands in front of their body hitting their hands together.

Sitting with slightly open legs is a relaxed position showing that we are comfortable. Also putting one leg over the knee of the other is a comfortable position.

Several years ago, I went with a couple of Chicago police officers to observe how they handled a domestic disturbance. A man had slapped his wife around and she had called the police. The Chicago police officer asked him to talk. The man was first sitting with both feet on the ground. The officer began the interview telling this guy he better watch out, or he was going to be arrested. The guy transitioned to crossing his legs and slowly started moving his foot in a kicking motion. Then his face went from a frown to a smile, and he told the police officer that he totally understood. He said, "You're absolutely right, officer. You're right, I really shouldn't do that." The officer nodded in agreement and got up and we left.

The Castle: Silent Communication

Looking at the transitions, did this guy really commit to stop beating his wife? The guy moved from a frown to a smile as he placed one leg over the other. His smile, I believe, was in relation to knowing he was not going to get arrested. One leg over the other meant he was comfortable with this decision. His foot displaying the kicking motion told me he wanted to kick the police officer out the front door. What do we think happened to the wife the next day?

This illustrates that deciphering body language is only possible when we see with our eyes and hear with our ears. I do not believe the police officer thought he made an impact. However, when we are talking to people and they display these types of transitions, it should alert us these people are not being truthful, and they are not listening.

When engaged in Verbal Chess it is important that we are aware of body transitions. Like watching the CEO in the sales meeting, they give us clues to what the opponent of Verbal Chess is thinking.

Clothing and Postures

Clothing is very revealing when it comes to someone's identity. Let's consider a young woman wearing too much makeup and a very tight, low cut dress. What is she trying to say? Let's also consider a guy with a big cowboy hat, a too big belt buckle, tight jeans, and cowboy boots. What is he trying to say? Let's say you're going to conduct an interview of someone applying for a job. He comes and sits down. His pants look like he has used them for a napkin, and his shirt collar is dirty. What are his clothes telling us about him?

Postures are also many times obvious. When I was an FBI agent in Montana, I worked a case of jewelry theft. The suspects were gypsies, who used the following method.

Consider the young clerk in a jewelry store when a woman came in with a small child to buy jewelry. She was well endowed, wearing a deep V-neck dress, and was constantly bending over the counter so the clerk could get a full view. While the woman distracted the clerk, the boy swallowed the diamonds. They exited the jewelry store without buying anything while stealing the jewelry store blind. It was much later the clerk realized he had been conned into watching her while the diamonds were stolen. The question that should have gone through the clerk's mind was why the attempt to distract? Then, should I set jewelry on the counter in front of her?

Postures can be very important when we are interviewing someone for a job, or when we are trying to get to the bottom of an issue. Posture can denote attitude, whether someone is tired, sleepy, alert, or not listening. Postures can also display whether people are aggressive, weak, strong, attentive, or do not care.

An open posture portrays positive emotions when hands, arms, and legs are relaxed. Generally, people with open postures are perceived as being more persuasive than those with other postures. A closed posture is crossing arms over the chest, crossing legs and possibly turning away, or sitting in a hunched forward position. These are all signs of a closed posture. On the other hand, a confident posture is standing or sitting fully upright, holding our head high, and keeping our gaze at eye level.

The Castle: Silent Communication
Psychological Synchrony

Researchers have found when we are confronted by an angry person our heartbeat speeds up and we literally feel the anger from the other person. This is like pointing our finger at someone. Likewise, researchers have found when we are confronted by an empathetic person our heartbeat slows down. Researchers call this phenomenon "psychological synchrony." It is a powerful reminder that the physical reactions of our minds, emotions, and bodies are intimately intertwined and interdependent on each other.

We have all heard the saying *love at first sight*. I believe this is when two people's heartbeats are in sync with each other and of course there is a strong attraction. This is a form of psychological synchrony. This indicates our empathetic mind/body response interacts with the feelings of our opponent's nervous system, commanding a like response.

Unbelievably, this does work. Let me give an example. When I lived outside of Chicago there was a husband and wife two houses down who were not our fans. One day, the neighbor's wife was jogging around the neighborhood and stopped to be polite to briefly talk to my wife. My wife's hands were on her hips and so was the neighbor's. This is psychological synchrony. They were both displaying arms akimbo. Again, psychological synchrony is a mind-body response that commands a like response, and they were both responding like each other. I decided to enter the picture and see if I could change the mind-body response. As I walked closer, both ladies stayed with their hands akimbo. I stood for a second with arms akimbo, and then changed to palms up, arms out gesture. The neighbor's wife immediately transitioned to using palms gestures. My wife wondered what the heck I was doing, but slowly changed her body language to neutral.

Psychological synchrony also works if we can change a person's body language mode. If a person is in a state of anger, if we can get them to sit down, this changes their manner. To demonstrate this, I was called to the entryway of the FBI office in Chicago and a man was standing there with his legs wide apart, arms swinging in front of him with one fist hitting the palm of the other hand. He was even rotating up on the ball of his feet gaining height. I gave him the palms up gesture with my arms slightly forward and out to the side, while asking him if I could assist him. My body language represented a normal non-aggressive honest stance. He almost immediately stopped swinging his arms, and I immediately offered for us to sit down in the outer office. Later I offered to go into the private office and sit down. He consented, and when he started walking with me, I could see the clerical employees take a sigh of relief. I twice moved him out of his anger body mode which changed his whole demeanor.

Psychological synchrony also works with the words we speak. I recently was involved in a situation where the man was so upset about a political issue that he was yelling at me. He wasn't listening, so I replied in a very soft voice, almost a whisper. At first his voice only lost an octave or two, but eventually he kept lowering his voice to the point of asking me why we were whispering. Yes, he was whispering too. I then reassured him, with positive body language and a sincere tone of voice that I would take the time to talk to him. He slowly relaxed and we had a normal conversation.

A sort of funny situation was a time when my teen daughter and my wife were arguing. I was studying psychological synchrony so I thought I would try it out. I asked both of them to sit around the table with me. Both complied but my daughter sat with both legs wrapped around her chair legs and her arms looked like they were tied in a not. She looked so funny; I couldn't help it. I burst out laughing, putting my hand over my mouth trying to stop. Remarkably, my daughter laughed, and my wife then laughed. My daughter said, "What are you laughing at?" between laughing sounds. I just shook my head no, still laughing. In a few seconds we stopped, then we all started laughing again. My daughter apologized and we all gave each other a hug. This is psychological synchrony in action. Caution: laughing seldom works, so be careful this can go from bad to worse.

Once we understand how to project kindness, concern, and empathy we have a very good chance of defusing anger and even violence, and most of all winning the game of life.

Personal Space[84]

All humans need physical space to live normally. "Halls Theory"[85] of personal space finds there are differences in how cultures use personal space, but the differences are small. Personal space changes depending on the situation, and the closeness of the relationship. It is used to communicate many different kinds of non-verbal messages and include signals of intimacy, affection, aggression, and dominance. Humans are territorial. Nations mark boundaries, properties are fenced, families sit in the same chairs, and we sleep on the same side of the bed.

One of the first items we are concerned about when we get a new job is our own workspace. Restaurant planners have done much research trying to psychologically design tables that will not be too close or too far away. Vehicle seats are designed so they are not too close together. Small sports cars have a console between the seats to make us feel good about sitting close to each other. Many refrain from buying vehicles because the back seats are too cramped but instead buy vehicles that are large and have lots of room. These are all personal space concerns.

All these distances are emotional barriers. Every human has emotional barriers implanted in their brains. This is critical to understand if we want to win at the game of life, Verbal Chess. The key to understanding these emotional barriers is simply becoming aware of the distances in which we communicate and then being very aware if we violate them.

Test your powers of observation by answering these questions:[86]

1. On the average how far apart do humans stand from each other?

2. Are there cultural rules governing how far we stand apart?

3. Most important, can we influence our opponent/client by changing the distance in which we communicate?

4. How do distances change our interpersonal relationships?

There are two combined answers to these questions. First, there are definite patterns to the way people use space to communicate, and cultural differences are normally small. Second, the distance we observe or ignore dramatically affects interpersonal relationships.

Recognizing Personal Zones

Personal space consists of the psychological space a person carries around with them as they move from one emotional barrier to another in our physical environment. This barrier is a kind of bubble that surrounds an individual and as people move through them towards one another or away from each other their relationship heats up or cools off. The following distances are generally where people operate:

- The intimate zone—contact to eighteen inches is where intense social interactions take place.
- The personal zone—eighteen inches to four feet is where personal social business is conducted.
- The social zone—four feet to twelve feet is where the impersonal social business takes place.
- The public zone—twelve feet to infinity is where impersonal meetings take place.

These distances are general and not to be looked upon as exact. When people are angry these zones expand in correlation to the person's anger temperature.

The intimate zone is where we are either very friendly or very angry. This zone is where I am yours, or I want to take you out. The intimate zone could be called the hot zone because this zone is for only intense social interactions. This is also the zone where the final step is taken before conflict.

Many of us have felt uncomfortable during a conversation because the other person was standing too close and invading our personal space. For the close talkers of the world, contact to eighteen inches is the area they cannot seem to stay out of. This space is reserved for intimate interaction, but it can also be used by an interviewer to heighten the interaction on-time, like I did with the electrical inspector.

The personal zone is the warm zone. It is reserved for everyday social business between casual acquaintances or for contacts interested in relating to one another in an intense fashion. When we meet strangers, for example, we stand in the far personal zone around three or four feet. This is the zone where we do the meet-and-greet dance. Okay, turn the music on, as we do one step in and one step out, while we shake hands and do the hokey pokey. This is the most common dance humans do.

The social zone is a cool zone. It is reserved for impersonal social business to symbolize that the parties involved are not interested in relating to each other. During working hours, for example, superiors commonly sit subordinates in the social zone by interposing a desk or table between the superior and subordinate. Their relationship is thus a formal work relationship. This is also the zone most of us like to be in if we want to listen to a presentation, or training.

Next is the public zone or the cold zone. It is reserved for very impersonal contacts, meetings, church services, courtroom work, etc. In this zone no personal contact is made. This is the back row of the room where many want to sit so they can go to sleep while the training or the church service is being conducted.

Warming or Cooling Interpersonal Relations

All communications, whether productive or destructive, are based on this general principle: moving closer heats up the relationship and intensifies the message being sent, while moving away cools the connection and dulls the emotional messages. Normally, friendly messages are intensified by moving or leaning closer and negated by leaning back or moving out to the distant zones. However, this is not the case with the intimate zone because moving into the intimate zone heats up the interaction.

Remember the CEO who was leaning back in his chair? This was a sign that he was cooling the connection and was becoming disinterested. Angry and aggressive messages are also intensified by moving in and weakened by moving out. The best practice is to increase the distance between you and an opponent who is displaying anger. Therefore, we can, whether intentionally or not, warm relationships by closing in and cool relationships by backing away to more distant zones.

Master the Theory

This theory is actually quite simple.

Step one: First memorize the names of the zones and the distances they represent. Then learn to estimate these distances accurately, but understand these are general distances—a few inches is not critical. Then practice the theory with your friends. One of the funny things I like to do is when a friend and I go out to lunch, I use the salt, and set it over next to his plate. This is their intimate zone; now watch the reaction. If nothing happens, when I put down my fork, I set it a little too close to them. If nothing happens again, after I take a drink, I set the glass in their intimate space. It is funny the reaction I get. I've had friends pick up my drink and put it back in my space and say, "What are you doing?"

Step Two: Control the messages we want to send about ourselves. Everyone involved in social interaction is constantly broadcasting messages about themselves through their use of personal space. Therefore, learn to diagnose the messages of others and monitor our own messages. How we use personal space is very important. Therefore, make our unconscious communications conscious. Do this by deciding what message we want to send—friendliness, warmth, or coolness—and send them.

Step Three: Conduct our interaction in the zone appropriate to the communication we want to take place.

Step Four: Maintain flexibility by changing the zone when the interaction needs a change. Behavior that occurs when two people are in the same zone seems to persist until that zone is vacated. It is also important that we warm or cool the relationships as required by deliberately moving into or out of a zone.

Step Five: Practice subtleness as we change the personal space in which we want to communicate. There are some situations where space is used to make an impact. In most everyday situations use personal space subtly or we will be seen as actors.

Please note: changing zone occupation is much more difficult if both parties are seated or if there are material constraints such as a desk or table. For meaningful conversations, it is best not to use a barrier. We Master Communicators want to see the whole body so we can see all the silent language. When we become proficient at changing zones in a subtle fashion, we will be able to channel our communication in a positive way to enhance the course of developing relationships.

Conclusion

The Castle is one of the most important pieces in becoming a Master Communicator of the Christian Art of Verbal Chess. In order to be effective fathers, mothers, employers, and employees, it is vital we become totally cognizant of body language—our own and that of others. Reviewing this chapter and practicing these skills will help make this part of your communication arsenal.

9

The Pawns

ON-TIME TECHNIQUES

A Time for Everything

"THERE'S AN OPPORTUNE time to do things, a right time for everything on the earth."[87] The Pawns in Verbal Chess are our on-time delivery tools or techniques used to move our opponent/client to persuasion or compliance through compelling positive influences. Pawns move ahead one space at a time. They are designed to be calming, persuasive, protective, and assuring, etc. but they do not move back. In the game of Verbal Chess, Pawns pre-plan, enhance, protect, and clarify. They are expendable, defensive, and enable us to take the offensive to win at Verbal Chess.

Pawns are created and delivered through our body language, personal space, tone of voice, and our words, while working in harmony with our minds, mouths, and bodies. Remember: regardless of what we do, if we don't absorb tension and project understanding through the Royalty of Verbal Chess, we will fail at being Master Communicators that speak life into others.

When we are talking to people who are angry, serious, excited, or depressed, we want to show concern, respect, dignity, and understanding. We do this both verbally and through our silent language within every Pawn or technique we use.

The Christian Art of Verbal Chess has thirteen on-time techniques: approach, personalization, assurance, clarification, forecasting, fact-finding, refreshment, praise, apology, swing phrases, appeal, story, and win/win Pawns. The Approach, Personalization, and Win-Win Pawns are every-time do. Understand that each Pawn's use varies depending on who we are conversing with and under what circumstances. When we are having a meaningful conversation with our spouses, we vary the Approach, Personalization, and Win-Win Pawn to fit the circumstances. The Clarification, Forecasting, Fact-finding, Refreshment, Praise, Apology, Swing Phrase, Appeal, and Story Pawns are used when the need arises and at the right time. I call these on-time techniques. The Pawns of Verbal Chess are intended to give us the necessary tools when the need arises. Learn to use these Pawns wisely, and the game of the Master Communicator will be filled with excitement and hopefully, fulfillment.

Approach Pawn: An Every-Time Do

The Approach Pawn is an every-time-do because it is critical that we start out every conversation correctly. Starting a meaningful conversation implies the outcome is important. We need to pre-plan a strategy and set realistic goals because without a strategy and realistic goals we are shooting from the hip. Past communication with an opponent should be reviewed. Realistic goals depend on the history we have with this particular opponent so we can design a winning strategy. Then we need to put on our resolve, which is the Royalty of Verbal Chess, a positive orientation of our minds. This will determine how we telegraph our manner, disposition, and emotions suitably to display the truthful feelings we want to communicate. We need this frame of mind to empower us to display an overall positive countenance. This is critical when we are going to have a meaningful conversation.

This is literally putting on our game face and it has crucial implications to the continuing communication process. We should try to be friendly, relaxed, and circumspect, but not threatening—and certainly, not uncertain. Success and failure can depend on how we start every meaningful communication.

Personalization Pawn: An Every-Time Do

Personalization is to make us more approachable. As we display a welcoming persona we are seen as open and engaging. We legitimately offer ourselves to the relationship. We may say something like, "Hi, I'm John, I'll be your sales representative today," while at the same time offering our hand. Maybe we need to discuss a problem with an employee we have known for several years. We may start with, "John, I'm glad you came in. How is your family?" Asking about a person's family with legitimate concern starts the conversation off on a positive note.

When we start a conversation by personalizing, we must do this with true sincerity. If in our heart of hearts we do not really care, go back to the Approach Pawn, put on our Royalty robes, the King and Queen of the Christian Art of Verbal Chess and start caring, and put on our game face. In our hearts, we need to be legitimately sincere. We cannot act because what comes out has to be perceived as sincere or we lose. I usually tell myself in these kinds of situations to exhibit mind over matter, or it will not matter.

The key is using self-control, then slowing down to give our statement weight. We may say, "How are you doing today?"

We wait for a response and commit to small talk. Or, when we introduce ourselves, we say, "I'm John," at the same time we are holding out our hand, making human contact in order to make it personal and legitimate.

When we personalize our introductions, we make ourselves harder to argue with and insult. We are now humans, showing we are not merely objects or a position. Even dealing with an old Billy Goat Gruff or a conflict starter, by personalizing, we become more genuine. This sets us up for positive communication.

Forecasting Pawn: An On-Time Technique

Forecasting is simply explaining the direction and purpose of our conversation or questioning. This is requesting our opponents concur with the logistics of the conversation—where we want the meeting to occur; if we will be standing, walking, or siting. This is not an every-time-do for every meaningful conversation, but under certain circumstances this is helpful if done on-time.

Here's an example: if someone comes into our office or home and our relationship is strained in some way, we may want to start by asking, "Do you mind if we sit over here?" or "Sir, do you mind if I ask you a few questions? Is that okay with you?" Or if we enter a place of business as an inspector we could ask, "Do you mind if I look over here?" Asking shows concern and respect. It also suggests we have no ulterior motives and confirms we are honoring them, their preferences, and their location. This is an excellent Pawn to use to show we honor others.

Assurance Pawn: An On-Time Technique

Assurance is a positive declaration intended to give confidence. This can be done by exhibiting the right body language or by determining our opponent's uncertainties and verbally taking them away. During a conversation when people go from uncertain to assured, they become reasonable.

Let me give an example: A bank customer discovers that someone has written a bad check against his checking account. The customer comes into the bank obviously very concerned. Immediately the teller recognizes the problem and gives the customer the assurance that she will to do everything possible to resolve this issue. Most customers then instantly go from uncertain to assured and can become more reasonable.

Assurance is the verbal sponge that absorbs tension without reproducing it. Only when we provide real understanding and assurance can we help a person see the consequences of their actions. Assurance is a positive declaration intended to give confidence that the uncertain can be resolved to the best of our ability.

Clarifying Pawn: An On-Time Technique

The Clarifying Pawn is a short, medium empathy question or statement during another's verbal exchange. They can be opinion questions, or questions trying to make something less confusing or easier to understand. As we learned, medium empathy questions are designed to gain insight. Clarifying shows interest and directs the conversation to a positive outcome.

Clarifying Pawns can deal with what I call "umbrella questions." These are questions with many possible answers. Only the speaker knows the main point they are searching for within the umbrella. The news media is particularly good at sucking a politician into answering an umbrella question so they can trap them. The person tasked with answering an umbrella question is thinking numerous possible answers, and many times wants to be polite and tries to answer. When asked an umbrella question, use a clarifying, or fact-finding question as many times as necessary to close the umbrella so only the main point of the question is revealed. In other words, shrink the possible questions down to the real point by using clarifying and fact-finding pawns.

When dealing with unsettled people, we should consider they are feeling stress. Opinion questions can lessen their stress allowing them feel affirmed because they know we are listening. Clarifying seeks understanding by projecting a caring person, while letting the speaker continue. These types of questions are many times short, sometimes one-to-three-word questions/statements during another's verbal exchange. If the speaker says, "I love living in Alaska," we may respond with a one-word question, "fish?" They answer, "No, I love the scenery, and . . ." "Mountains?" They answer, "Yes, mountains, and they are beautiful . . ." This example doesn't show enough time between answers, but it reveals the point I'm trying to make.

Clarifying seeks to understand, but it also directs the subject where we want to go. The Clarifying Pawn signals to the speaker that we want to know more and we are really listening. But be careful not to continually interrupt. Clarifying is a dynamic Pawn of Verbal Chess when used correctly.

Fact-Finding Pawn: An On-Time Technique

The Fact-finding Pawn normally comes after Forecasting or in conjunction with the Clarifying Pawn. Fact-finding questions try to determine the realities of a case, situation, or relationship by asking for specific data. Most people, after we forecast clarify, and don't mind answering fact-finding questions. The reason is fact-finding questions are concerned with practical matters and require only clear-cut answers: who, what, when, where, how, and why.

However, there are some questions, we do not want to use. They are like pointing our fingers. Questions like, "What do *you* know about this?" We learned in the Knight chapter to try to exclude the word *you* when asking questions. Also, we very seldom ask leading questions, because this is putting answers in our opponents' mouths; questions like, "You knew you were speeding, didn't you?" Both types of questions can be low empathy questions unless we use them after forecasting.

Fact-finding questions discover the purpose or get to the source. Direct questions (as opposed to clarifying questions) do more to get to the point and can lead to discovering the truth. Also, fact-finding questions can be used to obtain what is required to complete the interview or conversation.

Refresh Pawn: An On-Time Technique

The Refresh Pawn is the simplest Pawn to use. It is an act of charity, a small favor. It could even be a small, unexpected token gift, because almost everyone appreciates those. It could be a thank you in writing, or the purchase of a soda, coffee, or pastry. In the interview with the Indian woman, I provided sodas and chips when I knew she had been sitting in that jail cell for five or six hours. It is the easiest way to say, "I care about you personally." Through our benevolent actions these bits of charity speak louder than words. Also, the Refresh Pawn diffuses thoughts of hostility and sets us on a path to be understood.

Praise Pawn: An On-Time Technique

Offering praise communicates and reinforces our values. It increases our credibility regardless of our stature or role. It is the act of appreciating someone and showing confidence in their future. Praise then becomes positive for both past events and future expectations.

A little bit of praise can be a dynamic tool and a tension sponge. It's one of the oldest truths, "A person is praised according to their prudence . . ."[88] Like the story of my helper who I thought couldn't do anything right, once I found the good in him, I recognized his value, and he recognized his value. Then when I praised him, I set the expectations bar higher.

Nevertheless, praise has to be believable to work effectively. We must be sincere, focused, and authentic or we will look deceitful, like a bad actor, and kill the relationship. It is best to consider praise at the right time and place when we can make it sincere. It could be at the start of a difficult conversation, or when we are discussing an event that the person participated in which they achieved a good result. There is no doubt this can at times be difficult to do, especially when we do not care for the person. But the reward is worth it—a strengthened relationship.

Apology Pawn: An On-Time Technique

The power of an apology is wonderful because it solicits forgiveness. There are two kinds of apologies. First: *I am at fault* apology. This is when we know we are at fault and admit we are wrong. This is especially effective if we can apologize immediately when we know we have been wrong. This is when we feel, "The pain in our gut that keeps burning. I'm ready to tell my story of failure, I'm no longer smug."[89] When we acknowledge doing wrong, we telegraph to the world that we are not smug or arrogant. Truly arrogant people never offer a sincere apology.

This is important because people who are looked upon as smug and big-headed are handicapped during meaningful conversations. For example: a particular incident takes place, and we have received the wrong information. We have confronted someone, and they vehemently protested. It's not until later we discover we are wrong. Immediately, we should re-contact the person and apologize. This must be done on-time because an immediate apology maintains our status as the Royalty of Verbal Chess. If we delay people start to suspect our veracity.

The second type of apology is a vicarious apology. A person notices something is wrong and expresses a way to make it better; the person who has been wronged gets understanding and the hope for change. For example, a person approaches us and says, "You are always ignoring me." We answer with a question, "What makes you feel that way?" The accuser then says, "Every time you pass by my desk you don't look at me." We answer, "I'm sorry you feel that way, it was not intentional." Starting the apology with "I'm sorry you feel that way," is vicarious. The person who felt they were wronged obtains acknowledgment and is affirmed with a vicarious apology. This is a highly effective tool when we are dealing with sensitive people. A vicarious apology is when we don't have to make ourselves wrong to acknowledge a person's feelings and we maintain the harmony in our relationship.

A vicarious apology is not, "I'm sorry, but . . ." This type of sorry I call the "sorry butt" apology. They are really saying, "I'm not really sorry because it is your fault or someone else's."

A word of caution: if a person uses a vicarious apology too much, he is looked upon as a manipulating, unforgiving person.

Be very careful, and if you have done something wrong, apologize, and do it quickly and sincerely.

Swing Phrase Pawn: An On-Time Technique

The Swing Phrase Pawn or Questioning Pawn is a needed and skillful talent. In a verbal conflict or in a contentious conversation the swing phrase or, I could call it the Questioning Pawn is one of our most important techniques. This is the principle of controlling the direction of the conversation by refocusing our opponent, while appearing to be going along with them.

The Swing Phrase Pawn is more difficult to explain than it is to use. It is one of those techniques which, once learned and practiced, can become one of the best ways to keep from escalating or unknowingly creating confrontations.

Swing phrases usually have to be spoken on–time, meaning right after our opponent questions, insults, doubts, or calls us incompetent, and/or questions our heritage. However, the more frequent use is when we are simply questioned. This produces the majority of opportunities to use the swing phrase. When we are challenged, our first reaction may be to get angry or defensive, followed by the temptation to use low empathy statements. This is an immediate lose-lose and *we cannot* let this happen if we are to win the communication game of life, the Christian Art of Verbal Chess.

One of the best swing phrases is silence, especially in a group setting. When we ignore an accusation and leave it in space, this refocuses the warranted or unwarranted challenge on the speaker. Silence is one of most difficult swing phrases to perform. This is when we teach ourselves to not grab our insult-catcher's mitt; therefore, we do not catch the insult and throw it back. No, we must let it die in the vast universe of get back statements. This is what happened with the attorney when I was trying to explain the investigation and he went ballistic. Remember, I sat down—which shows respectful body language—and did not say a word. The CEO even apologized for him. Therefore, letting barbs, insults, and people's bloviating die in space is a great Swing Phrase Pawn, because the swing phrase is the sound of silence. I've learned it is hard to say anything wrong when I am silent.

The Vicarious Apology Pawn is another swing phrase we can rely on. "I'm sorry you feel that way." This statement can refocus an especially pompous person by validating and relieving their insecurity.

The following is an example of a deflecting statement that I do not recommend. When the aforementioned attorney finished his rant, had I said, "Can we get back to the task at hand?" Wow, this could have set him off. I would have been devaluing his point of view and displaying my arrogance for all the world to see. This is not a medium empathy statement; it is low empathy with a plus sign.

Let's recap: the Swing Phrase Pawn is used when we are under verbal questioning by an opponent. It is a short, medium empathy question or statement, which has the effect of making our opponents analyze what they are saying. These statements also affirm, because we are asking our opponents to speak.

Let me give a simple example. Someone says, "I heard you are saying untrue things about me ." Our medium empathy question in response could be, "You feel I'm talking about you?" This question is essentially denying the allegation by asking a direct question. The accuser says, "Yes, somebody told me you are saying some really bad things about me. What's your problem?" Now our question repeats our opponents' question in their words, "I'm saying really bad things about you?" We look perplexed, possibly showing palms gestures. The accuser: "Well, this is what I have heard!" Now they are questioning themselves, and it is time for a vicarious apology, "I'm sorry you feel that way." We have acknowledged the accuser feels he has been wronged. The accuser replies, "Well, maybe my information is not right." Now they are starting to second-guess themselves. Our answer could be, "I assure you, I would never purposely . . ." Here the accusing question and answer process is completed. We have taken their negative concerns, swung them around, and confirmed our positive position. Read this at least twice. We went to the positive position through medium empathy questions. This deflected the accusation, led them in a positive direction, and defeated the simple allegation by not disputing their assumptions but asking medium empathy questions. We deflected them or changed them to a new positive direction.

Here's an example of a bad exchange: the questioner says, "I heard you are saying untrue things about me." Our reply, "I'm not saying anything about you." We made the question into a statement and in fact, confronted it. This is low empathy. Confronting has turned the questioner into an accuser. He then says, "Oh, yes, you did. I heard it from others." Our start-the-fight answer, "You must be crazy or making things up!" Now we have confirmed their negative suspicion and are on the march to destroying this relationship.

Again, the best way to stop accusing questions is to start asking medium empathy questions. The ultimate swing phrase will allow us to pause almost anyone when they are verbalizing questions. The ultimate question could be, "Let me be sure I heard what you said," or "I'm not sure I heard you correctly." Then ask the question, restating their question in our words. This simple reflective or fact-finding statement is so empathetic, conciliatory, and sincere it shows we are trying to understand. Almost anyone will stop and pause so they can be understood.

Therefore, when opponents stop or slow down, we put their point or question in our words, and repeat it, sending it back to them for reconsideration. Then they have to listen in order to clarify our understanding of their question. We have now directed them to start listening and have gained their attention. Now we Knight them with additional paraphrased, medium empathy statements.

The swing phrase is simply inserting a third person (the one who does not understand) into the two-person conversation and asking an empathic question in our words with their meaning. The object is not to be totally correct in repeating their question. The object is attempting to understand by showing real medium empathy. In the last chapter, I will give several examples how this is used. The swing phrase empowers us not to "have anything to do with foolish and stupid arguments, because we know they produce quarrels."[90]

Appeal Pawn: An On-Time Technique

It is important for us to know how to appeal to people, because the right kind of appeal will help to keep them from doing something we view as wrong or troubling. People who need an appeal usually are exhibiting ulterior motives, or they are angry or irrational. There is an old truism: normal humans have one characteristic; if it is reasonable and self-serving, they will do it! Therefore, the best appeals are reasonable and self-serving.

Ethical appeal: these are principles of conduct pertaining to right and wrong. On one occasion I was testifying in federal court when the defense attorney started accusing me of some sort of impropriety. This is normal when the evidence is against the defense attorney's client. The U.S. Attorney stood up and said, "Your Honor, I object. This is an unethical attack on this FBI agent." The federal judge then told the defense attorney to abstain from any further accusatory remarks unless he had the evidence to back them up. This is the ethical appeal.

Personal appeal: this pertains to a particular individual. This appeal tends to be the most powerful. The question we need to ask is: are most people selfish? Yes! Make the appeal reasonable and self-serving and there is a good possibility they will do it. For example: a friend of mine was a coach for a Little League baseball team. One of the players' fathers lost it and started screaming at the referee. My friend walked over to the father and said, "John." This got John's attention. Then the friend made a personal appeal. He spoke in a whisper only John could hear and said, "This does not make us look good." John nodded and stayed quiet. The personal appeal is most effective between friends. The person we are appealing to knows it is coming from a friend. They also trust the friend's motives are correct.

Reasonable appeal: is not exceeding the limit prescribed by reason. Consider a movie scene where a woman fell out of the boat in a swamp. She started screaming, saying she was going to drown. Her arms were waving and thrashing the water. Another woman in the boat said, "Stand up!" The woman who thought she was drowning stood up. She was in about three feet of water. This is a reasonable appeal. My young granddaughter might call this a "No! Duh!", but sometimes reasonable is looking at the situation from the outside and seeing the simple solution.

Practical appeal: is being mindful of the results, advantages, or disadvantages of the final decision. A good example is when our family was taking a trip and someone had purchased one of the first GPS map devices to convey the right way to go. During the trip, we stopped at an intersection for gas. The GPS device said we should go in a particular direction. I was comparing the GPS with a real map, and discovered the GPS was recommending a way that included dirt roads. I offered a practical appeal, and we went the way of the printed map.

Story Pawn: An On-Time Technique

A word picture, or parable, uses a story to sow into the emotions and activate the intellect of our opponents/clients. This enables our opponent to "Listen . . . to what the story of the sower means."[91] This is the Story Pawn, which causes people to experience our words, not just hear them.

It has been said, a picture is worth a thousand words. If a picture is worth a thousand, isn't a story worth at least five hundred? Sometimes when we focus on a picture, we see the essence of a much broader meaning. I often look at a painting named *Mustang Mayhem* by Nicholas Trudgian. This painting is of one of the final air war actions of World War II. It shows the P 51 Mustangs of the fourth fighter group attacking the Luftwaffe airfield at Gablingen, Bavaria, 16 April, 1945. This painting is hanging in my office in front of my desk. I have studied this painting for hours, and every time, I see something new. This is the value of the Story Pawn.

The Story Pawn paints the picture of where we want our opponents to mentally focus. The story can be a few descriptive words or a short story; the object is the same (but avoid long stories or we will lose the essence). The purpose is to enable our opponents/clients to see and feel the meaning through the sensations the story will convey in their minds.

Story Pawns are painting words of empathy in such a way that they surmount the barriers of understanding, helping our opponents see the consequences of their actions. Word pictures, called parables, were used by Christ and today by coaches, sales managers, comics, parents, and cartoonists to inspire, challenge, warm, and make us laugh. Story Pawns are also used by Masters of the Christian Art of Verbal Chess.

We have some simple sayings that are Story Pawns. "He is as red as a beet!" This simple statement tells us somebody is embarrassed or has been sunburned. A Story Pawn was told to me by a realtor in Montana. I asked him how bad a particular dirt road was to a property and he said, "That road is so rough, you will need a four-wheel drive and a light lunch!" This very descriptive short story dispels any doubt in our mind that this road is almost impassable.

Story Pawns can be true stories or made up "what if" stories. A made-up story empathizes how bad something can become. A friend of mine and I were standing outside his home and I said, "Tom, you need new front tires on your vehicle." He said, "Yes I will get that done." His tone of voice was such that I didn't think he was serious. This is when I said, "What if your whole family is in your car, and the front tire blows out at seventy miles an hour?" He literally bent over taking a closer look and said, "Wow, I need to get those replaced."

I recommend every Christian Art of Verbal Chess player create a repertoire of stories to use. They are very effective and can literally save people from being injured.

Win-Win Pawn: An Every-Time Do

The Win-Win Pawn is simply the understanding of each other's position at the end of a meaningful communication. This is when we can agree or agree to disagree. It is a verbal arrangement, mutually accepted to bring together understandings. We are seeking harmony of feelings, or jointly owning the result. Do not misunderstand; a mutually accepted arrangement can be the parameters of a disagreement or agreement. It can also be when we are going to meet next and under what circumstances.

Ideally a win-win agreement is a state of synergism, the combined cooperative action used to increase each other's effectiveness. This can be as simple as friends agreeing to meet next month with their families for dinner. One friend wants dinner in April, the other friend wants it in May. They agree to have it on April 30.

The win-win agreement is also accomplished through reverse or reflecting paraphrasing with concurrence. Let me give an example: in California a friend of mine decided we were to meet for lunch at what I thought was Chevy's, and he understood it to be Chili's. On the date and time, I called him after I arrived at Chevy's, and asked him where he was. He said, "I'm at Chili's waiting for you. Why are you late?" I laughed and said, "I'm in Chevy's waiting for you, and you are late."

The use of reverse paraphrasing could have prevented this simple misunderstanding. Before we parted I should have said, "Let me confirm our understanding. We are to meet at Chevy's on this date at noon." This would have given us both a chance to confirm when and where we were going to meet.

The win-win agreement should be one of the last acts before concluding every meaningful communication. It is an every-time do.

Conclusion

Our reputation depends on how well we can skillfully manage our minds, mouths, and bodies, while influencing other people's behavior in a positive way. The Pawns give us on-time techniques; some we use every time.

The Christian Art of Verbal Chess as we have read has thirteen on-time techniques: Approach, Personalization, Assurance, Clarification, Forecasting, Fact-finding, Refreshment, Praise, Apology, Swing Phrase, Appeal, Story, And Win-Win Pawns. When having a meaningful conversation, we use the following Pawns every time: Approach, Personalization, and Win-Win. We use them every time to fit the circumstances. The Clarifying, Forecasting, Fact-finding, Refreshment, Praise, Apology, Swing Phrase, Appeal, and Story Pawns are used when the need arises and at the right time.

Use these Pawns and become proficient. Then you can develop your own on-time techniques to make you more skillful at being Masters of the Christian Art of Verbal Chess.

10

Pulling It All Together

CONGRATULATIONS, WE HAVE read and received instruction on how to become Master Communicators by using the Christian Art of Verbal Chess. We now know seventy to ninety percent more about communicating with our fellow humans than the average person. Presently we have been taught how to use all the tools in the Verbal Chess toolbox. We know their names, their uses, and what they look like, but we have not yet used them to build, repair, and enhance our communication skills. We are at the point of removing the nut from an engine block and trying to remember if we use an adjustable, closed end, or socket wrench. So, the question is: how do we pull all the tools in the Christian Art of Verbal Chess toolbox together and make them work to win the game of life by becoming Master Communicators?

Primarily we must complete the circle of wisdom. Wisdom has four qualities. They are: to know, to perceive, and to receive knowledge, and then, to apply this knowledge to the skills we have learned. However, before we can apply the skills to continue the circle, we must receive instruction—the essence of this book. Receiving instruction is accepting and learning the disciplines of a Master Communicator, especially the totality of the Royalty of Verbal Chess, which is being a person of honesty and integrity who is focused on giving grace. The circle grows as we receive, learn, and apply all the skills from the Bishop to the Pawns. The circle of wisdom is completed by knowing, perceiving, and receiving the knowledge of these disciplines and applying them to our everyday lives. In Verbal Chess we must "Walk in wisdom toward them that are without, redeeming the time,"[92] or we will fail.

The minimum mark of success in the Christian Art of Verbal Chess is after the conversation is over and our opponent leaves; they may not have agreed with us or been persuaded, but they leave viewing us with respect. We cannot control what other people think, but Verbal Chess is the ability to have the right motives which gives others the opportunity to see us in a positive light. Honorable motives are the foundation to being a Master Communicator.

Recap: The Tools of Verbal Chess

The Christian Art of Verbal Chess is played with character, dignity, and virtue, through giving grace to develop the art of speaking life into others. Without these attributes, we lose the verbal game of life.

KING—The Persona of Verbal Chess

The King is the mind and nature of the Verbal Chess side of the playing field, the moral compass, and the inner truth of who we really are. The King exemplifies ten essential character disciplines necessary to win life's game of communication. Emboldened by these character disciplines, the King designs the strategy and directs the pieces where they will do the most good.

QUEEN—The Skill of Giving Grace

The Queen is our most versatile piece and the most difficult to learn to use skillfully. The Queen works from within every piece on the Verbal Chess side of the playing field. It is truly the spirit of the game and is the power to impartially step into another's life, seeing the world through their eyes. Then selflessly giving mercy and compassion to gain understanding, while being able to step back and see the reality of the circumstances.

BISHOPS—Empathetic Listening

The Bishop is our intelligence gatherer, our unnatural, highly artistic tool to read our opponent. The Bishop can move diagonally across the playing field to search, anticipate, and understand our opponent's most important inner feelings.

KNIGHTS—Strategic Speaking

The Knight is our verbal personality and is the most unique motion piece of the game. It moves over or around our opponents to truthfully influence them. The Knight can be the key to success or an avenue to failure when playing Verbal Chess.

CASTLES—Silent Communication

The Castle is our silent vehicle of communication to understand what is *not* spoken and influence our opponent covertly. It also moves forward and backward, side-to-side, changing the playing field by presenting different views of our inner self and outward demeanor.

PAWNS—Our On-Time Delivery Techniques

Pawns use all the pieces of the game to move our opponent to persuasion or compliance through compelling, and positive influences. Pawns move forward one space at a time. They can be calming, persuasive, protective, and assuring, but they don't move back. Pawns are created and delivered through our body language, tone of voice, personal space, and our words, while working in harmony with our mind, mouth, and body.

Who is Our Opponent?

When we play Verbal Chess, we must realize our opponent can be ourselves or someone with whom we are having either a meaningful or adversarial conversation. Verbal Chess is not used when we are play-talking. Hence, the opponent can be anyone: a co-worker, a subordinate, a superior, a sales prospect, or current client. Also, our opponent can be a loved one, like our spouse, children, family, friends, or, someone we just met. Every time we have meaningful conversations *our motives* must be those of the Royalty of the Christian Art of Verbal Chess, displaying the persona of the King, (Christ), and skillfully giving the Queen's grace, (unmerited favor). Then we can use the Bishop, Knight, Castles, and Pawns to perfect the skills of being a Master Communicator to speak life into others.

How to Play Verbal Chess

The following are examples of invented conversations where Verbal Chess can be used successfully. They are provided as teaching aids. They are not exactly how these situations will necessarily progress and do not guarantee success or failure. They are merely examples and ideas of how to use all the pieces of Verbal Chess together, forming a meaningful and productive process leading us to become Master Communicators to speak life into others.

The topics for these exercises are as follows:

1. Conversation with the opposition

2. Adversarial situations using Verbal Chess

3. Conversation to correct behavior using Verbal Chess

4. Normal spousal conflict using Verbal Chess

5. Teaching and explaining conversation

Number One: Conversation with the Opposition

This is an invented conversation. The Pawns of Verbal Chess used during this Verbal Chess Game are the Personalization, Clarifying, Fact-finding, Praise, Forecasting, Assurance, and the Win-Win Agreement Pawns.

A state senator is told by his secretary, there are three ladies who are lobbying for a left-wing environmental group that want to meet with him. The senator immediately asks his secretary to describe their demeanor and if there is anything else about them she noticed. She replies that two are female, and the third is a male dressed as a woman and they do not look happy.

The senator immediately starts planning the Approach Pawn, reminding himself to put on his game face, and the Bishop, his listening hat. His strategy is to affirm them but not commit to supporting them.

Next is the Personalization Pawn where he will be friendly, making himself more approachable as he displays an honest, welcoming persona. His goal is to be open and engaging. Also, during the personalization he reminds himself to create a baseline of truthful body language responses. This, he knows, will be important as the conversation progresses.

Then he plans for Win-Win Agreement Pawn at the end of the conversation. He knows it is important to come to understandings which may be possible with just listening and not committing.

Subsequently, he looks at himself as they will see him. He is known as a conservative Christian. They will know he votes against all radical environmental laws. The transgender, because of his possible predisposition toward untrue judgments regarding Christianity, will especially notice if the senator treats him/her differently.

Other considerations he has are that he notices he has to be prepared to use the Swing Phrase Pawn if they push for commitments or make condescending statements. He nods to himself realizing he will use the Clarifying and Fact-finding Pawns. Then he reminds himself to control his own body language by continuing to present himself as open and not guarded. He reminds himself to put away his barb-catching mitt, and to stay with medium empathy statements.

He gets out a notepad and a pen, setting them on the corner of his desk, and walks to the door inviting the three ladies into his office. He immediately introduces himself and shakes hands with each one with a smile on his face and offers for them to sit around a very small table so he can visually see all their body language.

Once they get seated, he asks them to please tell him a little bit about themselves and with his open hand he first points his fingers to the transgender. He explains his background and doesn't tell the senator anything about himself, so the senator says the one-word empathy statement, "Hobbies?" He smiles because he has shown an interest. He tells him how much he loves skiing. He finishes, and the senator nods his head with a smile and looks to the next lady. She has picked up on the first person's replies and included her hobby of photography in her conversation. He makes a short statement that he also enjoys photography. Then immediately he gives the open hand gesture to the third lady to indicate it is her turn. This keeps the conversation moving. She finishes with her hobbies of motorcycle riding, and he nods with a smile, again indicating he also enjoys motorcycle riding.

He has remembered to draw a baseline of truthful body language. The transgender is exhibiting closed body language and is very guarded when giving his background. The lady in the middle seems to be the one in charge. She is very expressive showing a lot of positive body language especially when explaining her hobbies. The third lady is very similar to the second but has an interesting expression. When talking about her hobbies she gave kind of a crooked smile, and literally chuckled.

He then asks what he can do for them. The ladies defer to the one in the middle who obviously was the lead person. She starts telling how important green energy is to America. He makes several medium empathy paraphrased statements, and she is obviously affirmed and talks extensively. She then indicates to the woman on the senator's right that she had something special to tell him. He then leans forward just a little to show anticipation and gives her positive gestures and says, "Please explain."

This starts her explaining that drilling for crude oil and natural gas is no longer necessary in America. This is the point where the senator is talking to himself telling himself to control his own countenance and show no displeasure or negative body language.

He can tell that all three of them are looking for a reaction to the "drilling is not necessary" statement. They see no reaction and make a quick glance at each other. He purposely asks the woman speaking several questions to affirm her. (It should be noted, affirming someone is not agreeing with them.) This lady finishes her dissertation. The senator then goes to fact finding and clarifying, which their body language is showing they enjoy. The senator adds the Praise Pawn by seriously complimenting them on their knowledge of green energy.

The transgender shows a certain degree of discomfort. Therefore, because he has said very little, the senator pauses. The senator turns in his chair facing him, giving him attention, while slightly leaning forward saying, "Would you like to add anything?" She/he is slightly taken by surprise, but quickly a micro expression smile appears. He recovers, reverting to no expression, and says he agrees with the other two ladies. He then asks why the senator never votes for environmental protection bills.

The senator smiles as he notices the micro expression on the lead lady's face is a frown. He realizes this question was not in their script, and uses a Swing Phrase Pawn, stating, "Why do you believe I'm not for environmental protections?" The trans gives an answer that has no meaning in the real world. The senator replies, "That is an interesting opinion." (This is like a vicarious apology. The senator is acknowledging the person's feelings and affirms them by not disagreeing.)

The senator turns back to the lady in the middle and can see a micro on-time moment of relief on her face. The senator asks, "Is there anything else?" He successfully deflected the negative statement and swung the interview back to the positive. The lady in charge says, "I think we have covered about everything."

The senator stands signaling the meeting is over. He smiles fully and says to the transgender, "With all the snow this winter are you going skiing this weekend?" (Personalization Pawn) The transgender replies with a smile, "I'm going to try." He shakes each one's hand, looks them in the eye, and thanks them for coming to see him. He opens the door for them and smiles, while they exit. They walk out of his office smiling and talking, and he can hear the lead lady say, "I didn't know you liked skiing!"

A few minutes later the senator's secretary walks into his office and asks, "How did you do that?"

Number Two: Adversarial Situations

These are invented, possible conflict situations.

The First Situation:

Imagine you are a manager of a well-known restaurant. A new waitress comes and tells you a family of three has just told her the wife's food was served cold and the husband found paper in his food. She wants your help in dealing with them. What is your plan?

First use the Approach Pawn. This is when we pre-plan a strategy and set realistic goals. Ask the waitress the level of aggravation and using the Fact-finding Pawn determine the realities of this situation. (Note: try never to go into a possible verbal conflict without obtaining as much background information as possible.)

Plan the strategy. If the client is very upset, start with Personalization Pawn. Then quickly move to the Forecast Pawn and then to the Assurance Pawn to give the customer a positive declaration, right after the personalization. Then use the Clarify Pawn and move to the Refresh Pawn and then the Win-Win Agreement Pawn.

Example: Personalize the conversation by introducing yourself and state your management position which identifies you as the problem solver. Quickly use the Forecast Pawn, saying you are going to take care of the situation to their satisfaction. Then clarify the situation. Once they add or subtract from your explanation, this will affirm them. Then use the Assurance Pawn to let them know how you are going solve the problem. Then again use the Clarifying Pawn to get their concurrence. Follow up by offering them additional refreshment (Refresh pawn) especially for the child. Finally end with a Win-Win Agreement Pawn.

The Second Situation:

You are working at the walk-in counter in a bank, and an irate woman carrying a small child comes in and starts talking very loudly, using animated arm gestures. She is upset because there is less money in her account than she figures is correct.

Personalize the conversation by introducing yourself as the problem solver, saying you will assist her. Quickly use the Fact-finding Pawn to determine exactly what happened. Watch her body language and project a positive countenance to encourage psychological synchrony. Ask several questions and if possible, reduce her problem down to the smallest, clearest point. Pause the process long enough to use the Refresh Pawn to see if she or her child would like some refreshment. This shows you care for both the mother and child. Then use the Forecast Pawn. Say you are going to find out exactly what happened, then again go to the Fact-finding Pawn if necessary.

After you obtain the factual information, use the Clarify Pawn to review the situation with the customer. Once they add or subtract from the information, use the Assurance Pawn, and let her know the problem will be rectified.

Pulling It All Together

Once you have obtained the correct information and can identify the problem, use the Clarifying Pawn to gain her concurrence to the solution. End the conversation with a Win-Win Agreement Pawn, thanking her for bringing this to your attention.

Number Three: Conversation to Correct Behavior

You are a personnel manager and have to interview a supervisor who has abused his sick leave. What is your plan?

Chances are you know this supervisor. Therefore, you should plan your approach to be friendly but professional. Caution yourself on the use of your body language and focus on keeping the conversation as short as possible. Note: correction conversations that continue for an extended period can be piling on or beating a dead horse. It is likely the person you are talking to knows the reason for the meeting. Whether he does or doesn't know will affect your planning for the Approach Pawn, so this is important, especially if the goal is to keep the supervisor productive.

Use the Personalization Pawn sparingly and immediately go to the Forecasting Pawn. If the supervisor doesn't know about the issue of abusing sick leave advise him of the issues involved. Wait for an explanation and move to forecasting. Usually, conversations attempting to correct behavior are more productive when you start with the Forecasting Pawn. Example: "My expectations for this conversation today are to get past this issue and conclude with guidelines for future sick leave."

This type of forecasting relieves the pressure on the supervisor at the very beginning of the conversation and takes away many of the reasons for conflict. Then lightly touch on the issue by providing a simple to-the-point statement using the Fact-finding

Pawn. Then use the Clarifying Pawn to get additional explanation and concurrence with the facts.

If there are mitigating circumstances, briefly explore them with a Fact-finding Pawn. Then immediately go to the Praise Pawn where the supervisor's positive history is complemented. Finally, move the conversation to a win-win agreement that includes not having to address this issue in the future. Follow the person to the door, and again, in a professional manner, thank him for coming.

Number Four: Normal Spousal Conflict
Husbands

Your wife is aggravated at you for not taking your dirty shoes off before you came into the house. This has caused a big mess and it is the second time you have done this in the last two days. The real issue may be something else because she has been irritated about other things. You were hoping the whole thing would pass and be forgotten, but now you know she needs to talk about it.

The Approach Pawn is very important in this situation. Not only do you need to pre-plan the beginning of the conversation, but you need to remind yourself to exhibit the Royalty of Verbal Chess. In this situation we don't need the Personalization Pawn (husbands and wives are very familiar with each other) but we need to pre-plan the Win-Win Agreement Pawn.

It may be best to start out with a Forecasting Pawn, saying "Honey can we sit down for a minute, I would like to talk." Make sure you display sincere body language during the question and use the Apology Pawn quickly after sitting down. Do not use the "I'm sorry, but . . ." After this point in the conversation use the

Assurance Pawn (I will try not to do such and such) and then the Clarifying Pawn asking her how she feels.

This will enable her to start expressing her feelings. Use medium empathy, the Knight of Verbal Chess. Once your wife has started expressing herself, your best avenue is to immediately go to empathic listening, the Bishop. If there is a television or radio on, shut it off. This is the time for intelligence gathering to determine your next step. Identify the real issues, but don't be surprised if you do not understand them. Then, again use the Knight, medium empathy statements, but never the Anti-Knight. Keep control of your body language, the Castle, and show sincerity. Caution: If you think you are supposed to fix something, do not try. Men are normally the fix-it sex. Instead, empathize, affirm, and show a loving attitude, and the results of this conversation will be better than your wildest dreams. Remember, her greatest need is to be listened to and affirmed.

Wives

Your husband is not very talkative. The family vacation is coming up and you want his attention so you can make reservations. The last time you discussed the vacation it ended up becoming an argument.

The Approach Pawn and the Forecasting Pawn may be the most important Pawns to start a productive conversation with a male who does not want to talk. There have been studies showing men only speak so many words in one day and then they are done. Therefore, arrange a time early in the day when you cannot be disturbed. Using the Forecast Pawn, forecast the time and place to discuss your vacation and get an agreement.

Start the conversation by asking your husband what he would like to see or have as a family vacation. This may be totally different than your ideas. Use medium empathy clarifying statements to take his answers down to the smallest common denominator. This is where you define exactly what he really wants. During this part of the conversation use the Appeal Pawn and appeal to his family sensitivities. This is a good place for a Story Pawn of how your last vacation went and how someone else's vacation was possibly better. Even consider a vicarious Apology Pawn about the previous argument. Something like, "I'm sorry we had to argue about going on vacation."

Now, while in this part of the conversation, show positive body language, and try to get him to join you in authorship of the vacation, even touch on key personal experiences. Then use the Forecasting Pawn to clarify your next steps and, if he agrees, immediately move to the Win-Win Agreement Pawn agreement. Then use the reverse paraphrases of the Knight to get him to repeat the confirmed agreement. Finish by using the Castle; this is the only time I recommend touching his body with your body to cement the agreement. This man never had a chance!

Number Five: Explanation Conversation

This is an invented conversation. The Pawns of Verbal Chess used during this Verbal Chess Game are the Personalization, Clarifying, Fact-finding, Praise, Forecasting, Assurance, and the Win-Win Agreement Pawns.

I was sitting in Denny's one morning just after breakfast, reading my Bible, when a gentleman about twenty years younger than I, dropped by my table. He asked if he could sit down and ask me a few questions. He sat down before I could reply.

Then he said, "I was watching you read your Bible and I have a few questions, because I'm an atheist." That last part got my attention. Then I cautioned myself to keep control of my body language, the Castle. Note: I didn't have time to pre-plan this meeting, the Approach Pawn. So, I quickly went to the Personalization Pawn and focused on giving grace, The Queen.

I stated, "Before we get started, I want to introduce myself." I offered my name and hand and as we were shaking hands, he told me his name was Jim. I continued with personalizing by asking, "Jim, where are you from?" He immediately went to explaining how he grew up in Houston, Texas. Then I went to several paraphrased, medium empathy statements—the Knight—combined with clarifying questions. I obtained the following by paraphrasing.

"You grew up in Houston. "Family?" He never knew his father, and his mother passed away when he was eighteen years of age. He joined the army when he was eighteen and was honorably discharged after four years. He has had several jobs and now was working for a construction outfit. Jim seemed like a very nice guy.

He related that he used to attend church but got disgruntled with the people. I smiled and said, "It's always the people." He looked up and nodded. I said this truism to start our conversation with a medium empathy point of agreement. Thus, affirming him with the Knight. During this part of the conversation, I was watching his baseline body language, the Castle, and discovered he had a habit of turning his hand over to show his palm, while explaining a truthful experience. The conversation location was not ideal because I could not see the lower half of his body as we were sitting across from one another in a booth.

Then I volunteered an Assurance Pawn, saying, "I want you to know, I'm not the last word on explaining the Bible."

He said, "That is okay because I'm just looking for some answers."

"How can I assist you?" I said. (I used the word *assist*, because I feel it denotes a joint authorship, not superior knowledge.)

Jim looked me in the eye and said, "Why do Christians say they are born again?"

(I have noted in the Pawns chapter to beware of what I call umbrella questions. These questions have many answers, but only the speaker knows the point of the question or what they are searching for. The person tasked with answering is looking at an umbrella of possible answers. Therefore, when asked an umbrella question, use Fact-finding and Clarifying Pawns to shrink the question down to the real point of the question.)

So, I replied, "Jim, what exactly are you asking?" (I used his name because it personalizes.

Jim said, "I'm an atheist, and I shouldn't care, but how can anyone be born again?" (Note: normally when humans ask questions, and say they don't care, they care.)

"Jim, what exactly don't you understand?" (Fact-finding question to again shrink the question down to the real issue)

He stated, "A person can only be born once, so are Christians talking about some sort of reincarnation?" (Now I know the main point of the question.)

I used the Clarifying Pawn. "Well Jim, let me show you something from the Bible. Please read John 3:1-5, out loud, describing the new birth." [93]

After Jim read this Scripture, I asked him, "What does this mean to you?"

He stated, "This is saying, to be born again is to be born of spirit?"

"Yes, that is exactly right, the new birth is spiritual not physical. This is very important, so we have to have a clear understanding of what Jesus meant when he talked to Nicodemus."

Jim answered, "Do you mean, when He said, 'You must be born again?'"

"Yes, the new birth is as you said, 'to be born of spirit,' which is as important as our natural birth. Also, 'to be born of spirit' is not a figure of speech; it is a fact, a reality that carries eternal consequences."

Then using his truthful hand gesture, Jim asked the age-old question, "Then how does a person know he is reborn?" (This is when we use the Fact-finding Pawn.)

"Jim, obviously you are familiar with the Bible. Are you really asking how you can be reborn?"

Jim paused, looked slightly down and then away as he said, "I guess I am!"

Now it is time for politely starting a question with a Forecasting Pawn, then the main fact-finding question.) "May I ask, why do you want to know how to be reborn?"

"Frankly, I'm not comfortable in atheism and I want to know if there is something better."

"Since this is the case, let me try to explain being spiritually reborn another way. I will start with the most quoted Scripture, the one most necessary to understand. It is in John 3:16 &17.[94]

Will you please read this out loud for me?" (By asking Jim to read the Word of God it enabled him to feel its power.)

Jim picked up the Bible and read the Scripture. When he finished, he looked up and asked me, "So God gave His only Son so humans can have everlasting life?"

(Now the Praise Pawn) "Jim, you are very right," I said as I was nodding with a smile.

Then Jim turned his hand over showing his truthful gesture again and asked, "Is this all I have to do—believe?"

"Jim, belief is the first step of beginning your rebirth. First comes belief and then comes faith. Our spiritual rebirth starts with believing God gave His only begotten Son, that whoever believes in Him will have everlasting life."[95]

Jim started to speak but paused, looking like he had a question. Then he said, "I want to believe. Can Christ help my unbelief?"

"Jim, please read this where Christ says, 'The god of this age has blinded the minds of unbelievers, so that they cannot see the light of the gospel that displays the glory of Christ,'"[96] I paused and asked, "Now, who is the god of this age?"

Jim: "I suppose that is Satan."

"Yes, unbelievers have a barrier to overcome, because this evil world has blinded those who do not believe! Therefore, when you said, 'I want to believe, can Christ help my unbelief?' You opened the door to receive the promise of the power of God who turns the light on in our hearts. This empowers us to be able to see the truth of Christ.[97]"

"Wow," Jim said, "That is more profound than I thought." He paused and said, "I think I understand!"

"Jim, it comes down to this: do you believe God gave His only Son, so humans can have everlasting life?"

"To be totally truthful, I want to believe," Jim said.

"Jim, can you believe Christ dealt with this question?" I again handed Jim the Bible to read a Scripture where Jesus said, "If you can believe, all things are possible for him who believes. Immediately the father of the child cried out and said with tears, Lord, I believe; help my unbelief!"[98] I paused again for this to sink in.

Then I said, "Jim, Christ told the father of the child, all things are possible if you believe."

Jim said with a short chuckle, "If all things are possible, how can I earn Christ's help?" I did not understand the chuckle, so I continued by answering the question.

"Jim, you cannot earn salvation, in the physical sense. There is nothing you can do physically to earn salvation. God's grace cannot be earned because God's grace is a gift of both love and mercy. This is like standing before a judge who waved your sentence. He gave mercy to the guilty. Remember the Scripture, 'For God so loved the world so He gave His only begotten Son?'"

"Yes, I remember."

Now read this verse: "For it is by grace you have been saved, through faith—and this is not from yourselves, it is the gift of God— not by works, so that no one can boast."[99]

Jim, now looking serious, said, "I understand, I have to believe." He paused shaking his head; he was obviously struggling to understand.

I added, "Jim!" (I leaned over the table moving my opened hand into his intimate zone, The Castle, to make this important point.) "Your belief is the first step, and then comes faith. Let me explain. The Bible says, 'Now faith is confidence in what we hope for and assurance about what we do not see.' Then, 'by faith we understand that the universe was formed at God's command, so what is seen was not made out of what was visible.'"[100]

I continued, "Jim, belief is not visible; it is the beginning, the internal mind-controlled step to faith in Christ. Faith 'is the confidence in what we hope for and the assurance of what we do not see.'"[101]

Jim said, "I am starting to see. Then faith will come from the confidence gained through more understanding?"

We both paused for a few moments, then I said, "Please read this Scripture as Christ tells the world the answer to your question."

Jim read, "Pay close attention to what you hear. The closer you listen, the more understanding you will be given and you will receive even more."[102] Jim added, "Then if I pay close attention, the understanding comes from God?" Jim was looking at me for an answer when he answered his own question. "Then, I need to continue to learn to be given more understanding?"

"You are absolutely correct." (Praise Pawn, smiling)

"So how do I listen to have more faith?" Jim asked.

"Listening is hearing, but it is also reading, and reading is studying. When we study, we further understand. Therefore, we start with prayer asking God for the ability to understand."

Jim: "I don't think I know how to pray."

"Prayer is having a conversation with Christ and I recommend you do this alone. Just speak to Him as if He were sitting next to us, right here. Then read and study the Word, the Bible, and know God promised His Holy Spirit." Then I read, "He will guide you into all truth."[103] I paused to let that sink in.

Then I added, "The promise from God is the word of God, as written in the Bible, 'is living and powerful, and sharper than any two-edged sword,'[104] When you read the word of God, Jim,"—I paused for effect—"the promise is, God's Word will convict you of the truth, and help you change your struggle with unbelief into faith in Christ."

"I hope that is true," Jim said.

We paused for a long moment, while Jim was thinking, leaning back in the booth, looking at me, and nodding.

Then I said, "It is true!"

After a few more moments, I added, "If it is okay with you, we should meet next week to further this conversation." (Forecasting Pawn)

Jim replied, "Would that be okay with you? I think I can."

"Then may I ask, before we meet could you read the Gospel of John?" (Another Forecasting Pawn)

Jim replied, "I do not own a Bible."

"Okay, after we finish, let's walk to my car and I will give you a Bible. Also, I want you to know, when you read the Book of John in the Bible you will find there is not a more passionate, comprehensive, concise statement of the truth that tells you exactly what you need to know to have eternal life. Can you read it? It will only take about thirty minutes or so."

Jim: "I think I can."

"Here is my card, please give me your phone number." (Win-Win Pawn)

Jim said, "Okay!"

"Jim, let me tell you another bit of really good news."

"Ok, shoot," Jim said.

"You are embarking on a process of discovering not only the darkness where you have been living and are leaving, but the glories you are about to understand. All of what you will learn will astound you, and benefit you, and you will come to understand how to serve God as His disciple."

Jim nodded his head, as if he understood but I don't think he did.

"Now please let me pray and ask God to confirm your belief and future undeniable faith in Jesus Christ."

After the prayer I used the Win-Win Pawn, and reverse paraphrase to ensure the time and place of our next meeting.

11

Final Words

WRITING THIS BOOK, *The Christian Art of Verbal Chess*, has been a lifelong goal. The objective, as you have read, is identifying and learning the methodology of a Master Communicator, to develop the art of speaking life into others by creating a process that anyone can learn, practice, and grow to be proficient in.

I felt the best avenue for teaching the art of communication was as a strategy related to the game of chess based on comprehensive skills. The skills are the chess pieces: the King, Queen, Bishop, Knight, Castle, and Pawns. These pieces give the learner the ability to see the entirety of communication which makes the keys to successful communication easier to learn. Everyone, from the most intellectual, to ordinary people like you and me, can improve our powers of communication and learn to be Master Communicators to develop the art of speaking life into others.

This learning process was designed so the necessary tools of communication could continue to be practiced as we spoke, walked, and ran through life.

Therefore, associating life's most important game of communication with chess enables even those who do not know how to play chess, to learn communication is a game of strategy. To be successful at the game of chess, we have to plan the strategy by creating tactics based on the ability of the pieces of the communication game of life. ⁻

The Christian Art of Verbal Chess then becomes a learning process that helps us transcend the barriers to excellent communication by laying them out in front of us and simplifying them. We can now look down on the process of communication and see all the different pieces of the game we must master. This process empowers us to put tremendous value in our communication because now we can learn the game of the Christian Art of Verbal Chess in its entirety.

It is my hope and prayer that this communication learning process will enhance your life in every way to develop the art of speaking life into others. .

Blessings to you all,

Dave

Endnotes

1   Philippians 2:3-4 NKJV

2   My dear brothers and sisters, take note of this: Everyone should be quick to listen, slow to speak and slow to become angry, James 1:19 NIV

3   John C. Maxwell, *How Successful People Think,* Center Street, New York, 2009,page 51,52

4   Proverbs 21:5 NIV

5   Maxwell, page 53,54

6   Proverbs 27:1 NIV

7   Maxwell, page 53,54

8   Maxwell, page 53,54

9   James 2:12 NIV

10   Proverbs 19:1 NIV

11   Luke 6:45 NKJV

12   Proverbs 8:13 NIV

13   Matthew 22:36-40 NKJV

14   Matthew 7:16 NKJV

15   Matthew 7:12 NIV, So in everything, do to others what you would have them do to you

16   Galatians 5:22-23 NIV

17   "The Power of Personal Influence" — comes from *Self Control, Its Kingship and Majesty* (1905) by William George Jordan. https://www.artofmanliness.com/articles/manvotional-the-power-of-personal-influence/ Accessed May 18, 2021.

18   2 Corinthians 10:4-6 NKJV

19   Galatians 5:19-21NKJV Now the works of the flesh are evident, which are: adultery, fornication, uncleanness, lewdness, 20 idolatry, sorcery, hatred, contentions, jealousies, outbursts of wrath, selfish ambitions, dissensions, heresies, 21 envy, murders, drunkenness, rev-

elries, and the like; of which I tell you beforehand, just as I also told you in time past, that those who practice such things will not inherit the kingdom of God.

20 2 Peter 2:18 NIV

21 Jude 12 TLB

22 Proverbs 11:3 NIV

23 Proverbs 12:19 NIV

24 Ephesians 4:25 NIV

25 2 Peter 1:5-6 NIV

26 Matthew 22:39 NIV

27 Romans 12:20 TLB

28 Proverbs 11:2 NIV

29 James 4:16 NIV

30 Philippians 2:3-4 NIV

31 Colossians 4:2-4 MSG

32 Romans 13:9 NIV

33 Romans 12:18 NIV

34 2 Timothy 4:2 NIV

35 1 Corinthians 13:4 NIV

36 Colossians 3:13 NIV

37 Matthew 12:34-35, NLT

38 1 Corinthians 13:5 NIV

39 1 Corinthians 13:11 NIV

40 David Augsburger, Writer, Anabaptist Author

41 Hebrews 11:1 NIV

42 Proverbs 14:15 TLB

43 Isaiah 7:9 NIV

44 Matthew 17:20 NIV

45 Romans 8:24-25 NKJV

46 Tubthumper, Artist: Chumbawamba, Release year: 1997

47 Matthew 7:17-20 NKJV

48 Ephesians 2:8 NIV

49 James 3:17 NKJV

50 Revelation 17:14

51 Colossians 4:6 NLT

52 2 Corinthians 8:7 NKJV

53 1 Timothy 3:4 NIV

54 1 Corinthians 13:11-12 NKJV

55 Acts 20:32 NIV

56 2 Corinthians 11:19-18 NKJV

57 2 Corinthians 9:10 AMP

58 Colossians 4:6 NIV

59 Proverbs 11:25 NIV

60 James 5:5 AMP

61 Galatians 5:26 NKJV

62 Galatians 5:19-20 NIV paraphrased

63 1 Timothy 4:12 NIV

64 Proverbs 18:13 GNT

65 Proverbs 18:13-14 AMP

66 James 1:19 NIV

67 Proverbs 1:5 NIV

68 Matthew 13:14-16 NLT

69 Grace Adolphsen Brame, Theology Author

70 Ephesians 4:21-24 NIV

71 Proverbs 12:15 NIV

72 Ephesians 4:29 NKJV

73   Proverbs 22:11 NIV

74   Proverbs 17:28 NIV

75   Galatians 5:19-20 NKJV paraphrased

76   James 3:6 NIV

77   Colossians 2:2 NIV

78   Simon And Garfunkel - The Sound of Silence Lyrics

79   Proverbs 17:28 NIV

80   Proverbs 16:30 VOICE

81   Proverbs 16:30 VOICE

82   Mark 4:12 NIV

83   Matthew 6:22-23 ESV

84   Edward T. Hall, – *The Hidden Dimension*, Anchor Books, New York, 1969

85   Ibid.

86   Joseph C. Kulis, Ph.D.

87   Ecclesiastes 3:1 MSG

88   Proverbs 12:8 NIV

89   Psalm 38:17-19 MSG

90   2 Timothy 2:23 NIV

91   Matthew 13:18 NIV

92   Colossians 4:5 NKJV

93   John 3:1-5 NKJV- "There was a man of the Pharisees named Nicodemus, a ruler of the Jews. This man came to Jesus by night and said to Him, "Rabbi, we know that You are a teacher come from God; for no one can do these signs that You do unless God is with him." Jesus answered and said to him, "Most assuredly, I say to you, unless one is born again, he cannot see the kingdom of God." Nicodemus said to Him, "How can a man be born when he is old? Can he enter a second time into his mother's womb and be born?" Jesus answered,

Endnotes

"Most assuredly, I say to you, unless one is born of water and the Spirit, he cannot enter the kingdom of God."

94   John 3:16-17 NKJV

16 For God so loved the world that He gave His only begotten Son, that whoever believes in Him should not perish but have everlasting life. 17 For God did not send His Son into the world to condemn the world, but that the world through Him might be saved.

95   John 3:16 NKJV

96   2 Corinthians 4:4 NKJV

97   2 Corinthians 4:6 NKJV

98   Mark 9:23-25 NKJV

99   Ephesians 2:8-9 NIV

100   Hebrews 11:3 NIV

101   Hebrews 11:1 NIV

102   Mark 4:24 NLT

103   John 16:13 NKJV

104   Hebrews 4:12 NKJVcopyright © 2015 by The Lockman Foundation. Used by permission. www.Lockman.org
Scripture quotations marked ESV are taken from The ESV® Bible (The Holy Bible, English Standard Version®), copyright © 2001 by Crossway, a publishing ministry of Good News Publishers. Used by permission. All rights reserved."

Scripture quotations marked GNT are taken from the Good News Translation in Today's English Version- Second Edition Copyright © 1992 by American Bible Society. Used by Permission.

Scripture quotations marked MSG are taken from *The Message* by Eugene H. Peterson. © 1993, 1994, 1995, 1996, 2000. Used by permission of NavPress Publishing Group. All rights reserved.

Scripture quotations marked NASB are from New American Standard Bible®. Copyright © 1960, 1962, 1963, 1968, 1971, 1972, 1973, 1975, 1977, 1995 by The Lockman Foundation. Used by permission (www. Lockman.org).

Permissions